It's such a joy to know that my Father sees me as beautiful and innocent. It's such a challenge to become the person he believes me to be. This study gives me the discipline; Jesus Christ gives me the grace!

—Sherry Wright
Dallas, Texas.

Becoming Myself, Becoming His is a masterful progression of scriptures and thoughts pointing the reader toward a fuller understanding of the hope and treasure that God holds in store for each of us. Gone is the pressure to achieve and accomplish in order to earn approval; replaced instead with a warm welcome to personal significance in the eyes of the highest God! By allowing God's creative, transforming nature absolute control, the reader is set to mature fully.

—Lori Sansom
Searcy, Arkansas

Becoming Myself, Becoming His is transformational. The study connects us with our Father and King and teaches us to soar with confidence. It challenges the reader to live a full life free of self. Kay Watson has written a study for every lady everywhere. Out of her adversity, God is shining.

—Stephanie Bell
Montgomery, Alabama

BECOMING MYSELF
BECOMING HIS

BECOMING MYSELF BECOMING HIS

LIVING THE LIFE GOD DESIGNED FOR YOU

KAY WATSON

TATE PUBLISHING & *Enterprises*

Published by Tate Publishing & Enterprises, LLC
127 E. Trade Center Terrace | Mustang, Oklahoma 73064 USA
1.888.361.9473 | www.tatepublishing.com

Tate Publishing is committed to excellence in the publishing industry. The company reflects the philosophy established by the founders, based on Psalm 68:11,
"The Lord gave the word and great was the company of those who published it."

Cover design by Lindsay B. Behrens
Interior design by Jeff Fisher

Published in the United States of America

ISBN: 978-1-60799-478-7
1. Religion, Christian Life, Women's Issues
2. Religion, Christian Life, Spiritual Growth
09.07.06

"Now with God's help, I shall become myself."

—Soren Kierkegaard, 19th century

To Scott

For his endless encouragement

and support of this effort,

and to my parents, Jim and Arnid Caples,

for their prayers and loving advice.

Table of Contents

13	**Preface**	
17	**Lesson 1**	**Who Am I Anyway?** What Was God Thinking When He Created Me?
33	**Lesson 2**	**Sweet Dreams:** Does God Really Have a Plan For My Life?
49	**Lesson 3**	**Becoming:** How Can I Be Transformed into His Likeness?
65	**Lesson 4**	**What the World Needs Now:** Transforming Love
81	**Lesson 5**	**The God Who Smiles:** Transforming Joy
95	**Lesson 6**	**Sleeping Like a Baby:** Transforming Peace
109	**Lesson 7**	**Ladies in Waiting:** Transforming Patience
123	**Lesson 8**	**Living a "You-First Life" in a "Me-First World":** Transforming Kindness
137	**Lesson 9**	**The Difference Maker:** Transforming Goodness

151 **Lesson 10** **The Foxhole Friend:** Transforming Faithfulness

167 **Lesson 11** **Easy Does It:** Transforming Gentleness

183 **Lesson 12** **Get a Grip:** Transforming Self-Control

201 **Lesson 13** **Becoming Myself, Becoming His:** Personal Reflection

211 **Final Word**

213 **Further Reading**

217 **Focus Verses**

Preface

In the late summer of 2006, I entered one of the biggest transitions of my life. My son, Jarred, had just finished two years at the community college in town, and my younger son, Jordan, had just graduated from high school. The decision was made that Jarred would finish his undergraduate degree at Harding University, nine hours away in Searcy, Arkansas. He would leave home in August. Our younger son, who had been one of the top athletes at his high school, hoped to play college football. After much consideration, Jordan decided to attend the same university that his older brother had selected. He too, would leave in August. Overnight my world changed dramatically! I had never known anyone whose children all left home on the same day! After almost twenty years of being someone's mother, I suddenly found myself searching for how to switch hats and be just Kay. I was still a wife, but my day-to-day routine was about to be completely changed. How would I adjust to planning my day according to ... well, whatever I wanted to do instead of what was going on with the boys? Despite the fact that it would seem only natural, I found it quite the opposite. I finally had the opportunity to ask myself, "What is it that you really want to do with your life?" This Bible Study evolved as an outgrowth of my experience.

Soren Kierkegaard, the nineteenth-century Danish philosopher, has set the tone for this study with these words— "Now with God's help, I shall become myself." We cannot truly be ourselves in the way that God intends without his divine empowerment. As women today, we find it next to impossible to discover who it is that God created us to be between carpools, loads of laundry, PTA meetings, and working outside the home. Even those who are not employed are finding it increasingly burdensome to manage today's busy family and maintain their spiritual identities. Finding the time for self-assessment, goal setting, and spiritual renewal seems like a pie-in-the-sky dream. We can only hope that one day, when things settle down, we will have time to work on our relationship with God.

It is my hope and prayer that through this Bible study, women will find themselves better equipped, not only to manage life, but to live it to the fullest, as Jesus taught. In addition, I pray that they will begin to fully realize the beautiful women God intended for them to be.

How to Use This Book

This study can be used in a number of ways. As a personal Bible study, each lesson should be completed over a three-day period. The **Focus Verse** should be used as a memory verse. The **For Additional Study** section is provided for an optional fourth day of study.

For a group Bible study, the participants should complete the lessons prior to attending the group session and then share their experiences and thoughts together in the group setting.

The Fruit of Spirit from Galatians 5:22–23 will be examined as the basis for study on the pursuit of holiness and transformation. Days one and two of each lesson are filled with Scripture study and thought-provoking questions related to the week's topic. Practical suggestions for training in these nine growth areas are included in day three of each lesson. These holy habits will serve to increase our effectiveness and our Christian witness. A **Focus Verse** of Scripture is provided at the beginning of each lesson. This is intended for meditation and memory work. (All of the verses are printed and included at the end of the book for tear out.) Each lesson concludes with a prayer of thanksgiving and request for strength to overcome obstacles that would hinder us from becoming his.

God bless you as you begin this Bible study. May you come to know yourself and your heavenly Father in a new and deeper way!

LESSON 1

Who Am I Anyway?

What Was God Thinking When He Created Me?

FOCUS VERSE

Psalm 139:23-24

Search me, O God, and know my heart; test me and know my anxious thoughts. See if there is any offensive way in me, and lead me in the way everlasting

This week our study will center on the loving attention God gives to each of us all the days of our life. His careful consideration to our physical form as well as his patient, guiding hand throughout our days confirms that we are his heart. He invites us to witness his glory as he works out his perfect plan in our lives.

Day 1

Fearfully and Wonderfully Made

Who are you?

How would you answer that question? I don't mean what relationships you have or what you do everyday. Who are you? If you were to describe the person who is reading this right now, without using any functional nouns like mother, wife, secretary... what would you say?

____

____

We often find it hard to give an answer to that question. It seems that as women, we are so tied to the roles that we play within our families or our vocation that it is difficult to know who we really are deep inside. The truth is we don't often have time to ponder the question. Our days may be so filled with activity and service that we seldom take the time to ask ourselves who it is that God created us to be.

One thing is certain. Whether we have it completely figured out or not, there is one who knows us intimately. This week's lesson is designed to point out just how much we are each loved by God and how he desires a closer relationship with each of us. Yes! God knows us, and he loves us just the way we are! Each one of us is a unique work of God—a masterpiece with his fingerprints all over us. What's that? You say you don't feel like a masterpiece? Well, you have got a treat in store with our Scripture study today. I think you'll be surprised to see that God delights in you and is eager for you to bare your soul to him each and every day. He waits for you! Sit down and grab your Bible, a pencil, and maybe even a cup of tea. Spend the next few minutes enjoying the truths from God's word concerning *you!*

Read the entire 139th Psalm. Read it slowly and celebrate each verse's affirmation of your Father's love.

As you read this, can you hear the thanksgiving and sheer delight in David's soul over God's divine knowledge of him?

Read verses 1–4 again. Describe what this kind of attention to your life means to you.

God Almighty has made it a priority to know all about us. He takes an interest in where we are and what we do. He knows us even better than we know ourselves. Even the thoughts that are yet to be vocalized or even to be understood by us are under his consideration. He knows the good and the bad within us and never misjudges us. He sifts the wheat from the chaff and remembers that we are but dust. God never ceases to be with us, whether we acknowledge his presence or not.

Consider verses 5 and 6. What does it mean, "You hem me in—behind and before?"

The great theologian, Charles Spurgeon, describes it this way in his *Treasury of David Commentary:* "Behind us there is God recording our sins, or in grace, blotting out the remembrance of them; and before us there is God foreknowing all our deeds and providing for all our wants." To put it in today's language, God has your back.

What is David's reaction to this knowledge?

Satan wants us to believe that our everyday, humdrum activities are too insignificant to bother the

Lord with them. He would tell us that God could care less whether or not we are able to balance our bank statement or whether we get all our shopping done for dinner tonight. Right? Wrong.

What does 1 Peter 5:7 have to say about that

____

____

All means all!

Now, revel in verses 7–12 for a moment. These thoughts should not promote a feeling of anxiety or fearfulness in you. They should bring great comfort in knowing that we are never out of God's "jurisdiction." He is always close by to lead us and sustain us. Wow!

To quote Charles Spurgeon once again:

Darkness and light in this agree;

Great God, they're both alike to thee.

Thine hand can pierce thy foes as soon

Through midnight shades, as blazing noon.

Verses 13–16 paint a beautiful picture of the care and thought that were in the mind of God at the time of your conception. Read them again.

How much more we now know about the workings of the human body than did the psalmist, and yet he knew enough to marvel at the intricate functions at work within him. It aroused in him great admiration and awe. It's as if God had the plan for our form and shape written in a sketchbook to be completed at the proper time. He knew that he was fashioning a body that would one day house his Holy Spirit. The concept described here as *knitting* is such a personal one. It implies a great attention given to detail, precision, and careful manipulation of material. Double wow!

The Hebrew word for unformed body in verse 16 can be translated as *embryo.* Is there any doubt when life begins in God's eyes?

In verses 17 and 18, David expresses his sheer delight and intrigue at the vastness of God's knowledge. He likens the thoughts of God to the grains of sand on the seashore.

Why do you think David asks the Lord to search his heart in verse 23?

____

____

What "offensive ways" might the Lord find in your heart today?

____

____

Write the **Focus Verse** for this week on the lines below. Commit to memorize it during the coming week.

____

____

____

In a sentence, express your feelings to your Father concerning all that we have studied today.

____

____

____

____

I hope that it is crystal clear from our lesson today that your Father in heaven loves you infinitely more than anything you've experienced on this earth. He is your biggest admirer!

Let the words of our **Focus Verse** be your prayer as we close our study today.

Day 2

God's Woman

Well, it's pretty clear. There's more to you than meets the eye. God made someone very special when he fashioned you in your mother's womb. You are a soul who will live for eternity, created in the image of the Most High God, fearfully and wonderfully made, and loved beyond measure.

Weren't those words of David from Psalm 139 beautiful? Just think; the same God who created the universe takes such an interest in you! The premise of this study is to discover how we can become who we were created to be through Christ Jesus. In becoming his woman, we become our true self. We learn to experience the happy, peaceful, and abundant life we were created for. Just like the message on the box, however, "some assembly is required." We must cooperate with God in discovering his divine plan for our lives. Consider the words of the rhyme below taken from *Every Life is a Plan of God*, by J. Oswald Sanders.

Behind the scenes where we cannot see,

A hand divine works the things that be,

And brings to my path the scheme devised

By the maker of earth who built the skies,

But he leaves to me to choose the life he plans,

Or to walk the way of self's demands,

To build on the rock or the sinking sands.

Our **Focus Verse** for this week is such a great tool for helping us to become God's woman. I hope that those words will become your daily prayer as you continue through this study. What a tragedy for sin to remain hidden in our hearts, undiscovered. Jesus our Savior waits to disclose any offensive way in us and cleanse us completely with his loving hands.

Why is it often difficult to be the women of God that we desire to be?

____

____

____

What do you perceive as your greatest spiritual needs presently?

____

____

____

Isn't it a comfort to know that we do not embark on this journey alone? God's desire is to walk with us and direct our path.

Take a look at a few of the promises from God's word that we can claim as our own. Fill in the missing words.

Psalm 25:8, 9
"Good and upright is the Lord; therefore he __________________ sinners in his ways. He ______________ the humble in what is right."

Psalm 32:8
"I will __________________ you and _______________ you in the way you should go; I will _____________________ you and _______________ over you."

Psalm 48:14

"For this God is _____________ _____________ forever and ever; He will be our ______________ even to the end."

Isaiah 58:11
"The Lord will __________________ ___________ _________________; he will satisfy your ____________________ in a sun-scorched land and will __________________________ your frame. You will be like a __________ _________________ __________________, like a spring whose waters never fail."

Describe how these words make you feel.

____

____

____

It is clear that our heavenly Father is patient and willing to teach us to be the women he desires us to be.

I always appreciate reading about all the purely human characters in the Bible. Jesus ministered with a group of twelve men who were not at all certain of what God's plan for their lives really was. We know for a fact that they had it all wrong. And yet once the Holy Spirit came to dwell within them, they were able to cooperate with the Father and allow God's plan for them to play out. These ordinary men were able to be used in a mighty way to help establish his kingdom on earth.

Jesus said to them on the occasion of his washing their feet, "You do not realize now what I am doing, but later you will understand." God reveals things to us in his good time. We must have ears and hearts that are open to hear his voice.

Are you ready to cooperate with God to realize your full potential in Christ?

What does Deuteronomy 29:29 have to say concerning the secret things of God?

____

____

____

We know that God's word tells us that if we listen we can hear the voice of God (Psalm 16:7, Isaiah 30:21, John 10:27). When is the last time you intentionally stopped to listen for the voice of God? In what ways does he speak to us today?

____

____

____

If we have not heard from the Lord in a while, maybe we need to reevaluate our quiet times. Are we spending all our time talking to God but not listening for his reply? Maybe we have never asked him to "search us and test us." Are we afraid of what he might tell us?

What is the difference between accomplishing things for God and allowing him to accomplish his work through us?

____

____

What do the following Scriptures have to say concerning God's work in our lives?

Isaiah 26:12

____

____

Isaiah 64:8

____

____

____

Jeremiah 18:6

____

____

____

We see from Scripture that God's earthly pool of prospective workers was flawed. He had (and still has) only imperfect vessels to work with. However, we know that with his divine molding and shaping he can do the miraculous through the mortal.

Who were some unlikely "heroes" in the Bible?

____

____

____

Knowing the great works that God accomplished through these flawed vessels should remind us that we can be used for divine purposes as well.

As we close today, pray that God will soften your heart and open your ears to his voice. In our next lesson, we will look at an amazing event in the life of Moses that will inspire you to seek the Father's presence in a whole new way.

Day 3

Seeing His Glory

I hope that our study this week is beginning to strike a chord in you that you are special to God. He wants to use you for the most important work on this earth, glorifying his name. He knew you even before you were born and all of your days are written in his book. Even the hairs on your head are known to him. All you have to do is be a willing participant in his divine plans.

How is the memory work coming? Continue to review this week's **Focus Verse** and use it as a regular part of your time with the Lord.

Today we will consider how we might better learn to appreciate his presence and follow his lead.

Our text for today's lesson is from Exodus 33. You will remember that God had commissioned Moses to lead his people, the nation of Israel, out of Egyptian bondage and into a new and promised land. After leaving Egypt, the Israelites made their way into the desert. God had instructed Moses to create a tabernacle for worship and had called him up to Mt. Sinai to receive the law. While Moses was away, the people began to grow impatient and encouraged Aaron to build them a golden calf that they might worship it. Upon Moses' return, with the tablets of the law in hand, Moses became outraged at the people's unfaithfulness. After seeing that three thousand of the people died that day for their sins, Moses felt discouraged about his calling. Let's pick up the story in verse 12 of chapter 33. Read through the end of the chapter.

From the tone of Moses' words in verse 12, describe how he must have been feeling.

____

____

____

What confirmation does Moses ask for? (v.13)

____

What bold statement does he make to the Lord?

Moses reminds God that this endeavor was his idea. He seeks guidance and strength to accomplish the seemingly impossible task of leading a nation of forgetful, ungrateful, and unruly people. Moses asks the Lord to teach him his divine ways so that he may know the Lord.

The primitive Hebrew root word for "know" is *yada'* (pronounced- yaw-dah'), meaning *to ascertain by seeing.*

Moses asks to see the Lord.

How does God answer Moses?

We know that God made his presence known to his people in the form of a pillar of cloud. Whenever God would speak to Moses, the cloud would remain visible at the tent of meeting.

What does Moses further request in verse 18?

Now read verses 19–23 again, and try to appreciate God's tenderness with Moses.

What did God do for Moses?

Why do you think God humored Moses in this request?

I do not believe that God is in the business of physically passing before us or audibly speaking to us today as he did with Moses. However, I am certain that he wants to show us his presence. He longs for us to see him everyday—at work and in our private world. He desires to carry out the plan that he designed for us even before we were born.

Has God passed by you lately?

Are you watching for him? Do you live with the expectation that he is at work in your circumstances? Do you acknowledge his intervention in your successes? Has he sent special help or comfort to you lately through a song, a scripture, or a friend? Stop and consider if God passed by you lately.

The apostle Paul reminds us in Philippians 1:6 that "He who began a good work in you will carry it on to completion until the day of Christ Jesus." Let him!

As we close this week's study, prayerfully consider God's great love for you. Remember that you are fearfully and wonderfully made. Look into that mirror and see the woman God created. She's an original, signed with the finger of God.

Be blessed this week, sisters!

Dear Father in heaven,

What an awesome God you are! I thank you for creating me in your very image. Help me to better understand your great love for me, both in my unique design and in your beautiful plan for my salvation. May I accept the gracious blessings you have bestowed on me, and in turn, live to be a blessing to others.

In the Name of Jesus,

Amen

For Additional Study

Read the following Scriptures and record what each one has to say about our Father in heaven.

1 Samuel 2:2–3

____

Psalm 44:20–21

____

Psalm 55:22

____

Psalm 94:11

____

Nahum 1:7

____

Matthew 6:8

____

LESSON 2

Sweet Dreams:

Does God Really Have a Plan for My Life?

FOCUS VERSE

Jeremiah 29:11

"For I know the plans I have for you," declares the Lord, "plans to prosper you and not to harm you, plans to give you hope and a future."

Looking Back

I hope our last lesson inspired you to think differently about your relationship with God. Did you allow the words of our **Focus Verse** (Psalm 139:23–24) to take root in your heart? Have you committed it to memory? Have you found yourself asking God to search and know you (and really mean it)? Today's lesson promises to be a shot of vitamin B-12 for the soul. It's all good news!

Day 1

Divine Dreams

It's true, you know. God does have a sweet dream for your life. You are his heart. He gave up his very Son for you. You can be sure he has special plans for your life.

Encourage yourself with a few more examples of God's love for you.

Write down one or two key words from each verse.

Matthew 7:11

____

1 John 3:1

____

1 Corinthians 2:9

____

2 Chronicles 16:9a

____

James 1:17

____

Have you ever considered what the Lord might have had in mind for you when he created you? Did he give you a certain gift or gifts to be used for his glory?

Of course he did!

Go back to the writings of David. Fill in the blanks below.

Psalm 138:8 "The Lord ____
__________ __________ . . ."

The New Testament also bears out this truth. Complete the following verse:

Ephesians 2:10 "For we are ________ ________________, created in Christ Jesus ______ ________ ______________ ____________ which God prepared in advance for us to do."

We studied in the last lesson about God's personal interest in each one of us. Understanding that God made you for a purpose is crucial if you intend to yield yourself to his will for your life.

Zig Ziglar, the internationally known author and speaker, poses this question:

"Are you a wandering generality or a meaningful specific?"

Let that sink in a moment. Do you wander around aimlessly trying to discover where your place is, or do you have in mind a purpose and a mission for your life? If God decides to, he can use whomever he chooses to accomplish his plans, but a woman who knows her purpose is more easily used than one who sees no direction in her life. Often the busiest woman in town is simply a wandering generality. She has not discerned the mission God has in mind for her. She may feel the need to be a part of every good work she sees going on around her. (Notice I said "good" work.) This usually renders her a frazzled, unfulfilled, and ultimately burned-out mess.

Do you know the good work God has planned for you to do?

____

It may be one thing for a time, and then he may have in mind a different area of service later on. God is so good. He allows us to grow and as our stage of life or interests change, he gives us new work to do in those places. It is certain, however, that God expects us to work within the boundaries of the talents that he gives us.

It takes reflection, prayer, and often feedback from others to discern what it is God would have us join him in. To quote Anne Murchison: "What many will miss in activity, God will reveal in prayer."

There is no better example of God's divine plan for a life than in that of Joseph in the Old Testament. Turn to the thirty-seventh chapter of Genesis. Read carefully the first eleven verses. Look for God's fingerprints on Joseph's young life.

What was the first sign of God's call on Joseph's life?

____

None of the family cared much for Joseph's dreams.

What does it say about his father, Jacob, in verse 11?

____

For some reason, Jacob just couldn't discount Joseph's words completely. Maybe he was remembering what the Lord had told him years earlier.

What was God's promise to Jacob in Genesis 35:11–12?

____

____

Of course, you remember that Joseph's days were not all easy ones. Often God finds it necessary to do a little fine tuning before he can put his plans for us into motion.

What about Joseph might God have needed to "tweak" before he could use him?

____

What were some of the major trials that Joseph endured on his way to Pharaoh's side?

Genesis 37:19–28

____

Genesis 39:1, 4, 6–20

____

Genesis 40:9–23

____

____

How did Joseph respond in each of these trials?

____

____

Read Joseph's gracious statement to his brothers in Genesis 45:5–9.

What a gift that must have been to Joseph's brothers. In Genesis 50:20, Joseph told those who had so badly mistreated him: "You meant it for evil, but God meant it for good."

Joseph was not immune to disappointment or heartache, even though we see no indication that he ever stepped outside of God's will. Each trial that God allowed Joseph to endure served only to make him stronger and better prepared for the task that lay ahead.

What comforting words appear again and again throughout the story of Joseph? Genesis 39:2, 39:21, 39:23

____

____

Just as God used Joseph to save a mighty nation, he has in mind to use you, his precious daughter, for his purposes. Believe it!

Day 2

Discovering the Gift

Have you ever imagined your own story written in the Bible? Remember those blessed words from Genesis 39:2, 21, 23 concerning Joseph: "The Lord was with Joseph and he prospered ... The Lord was with him and showed him kindness and granted him favor ... The Lord was with Joseph and gave him success in whatever he did." Can you imagine those words written in regard to your life?

"And the Lord was with ___________________, and she prospered."
(Insert your name)

Or "The Lord was with ___________________ even through a difficult situation, and he showed her kindness and granted her favor."

And how about "God took care of ___________________ and provided for her needs all the days of her life."

The Apostle Paul's words to the Romans encourage us to continue hoping in the Lord even in the face of trials. Write Romans 12:12.

____

____

____

Joseph persevered and was blessed for it. I hope we don't miss those beautiful blessings within the trials. Sometimes it's difficult to see the Lord's hand on us when we struggle, but with God's grace we will be able, as Joseph did, to look back and see that, indeed, the Lord is with us, and we will prosper.

There is a story of a young man who left the old country and came to America to begin a new life. Before he left, his father gave him a small amount of money to tide him over until he could get a job. His mother handed him a box containing homemade sandwiches, fruit, and other food items to sustain him on the long journey. They kissed him goodbye and sent him on his way.

Once on the boat, the young man gave the porter his ticket and found his way to his tiny cabin. When mealtime arrived, the young man opened up one of the wrapped sandwiches and ate silently at one of the vacant tables in the dining car. Most of the other passengers were laughing and enjoying what smelled like a delicious meal set on tables which were adorned with nice linen tablecloths. The young man smiled politely and continued with his sandwich. He offered a silent blessing on his beloved family back home.

After many days at sea, the young man's food supply was growing slim. He smelled the aroma of the cooked meals each day, and his stomach rumbled with hunger. He began to ration himself to a few crackers and some cheese each day. He even resorted to drinking rainwater he had collected in a cup.

Finally, when he had nothing else to eat and three days of traveling to go, he gathered the courage to approach the porter. He pointed to the delicious meal of a fellow passenger and, in broken English, said, "How much?" The porter looked confused and shook his head. He replied, "It costs nothing, my boy. You are free to eat."

How unfortunate that the young lad had settled for dried cheese and stale crackers when he could have been feasting at a magnificent table! He settled for the life of a pauper when he could have dined like a prince.

What is even more unfortunate is when we fail to live the blessed and beautiful life that our Father intends for us. We settle for a hurried and frazzled existence rather than allowing ourselves to enjoy a rich fellowship with Christ and the blessings he has in store for us.

The truth is God has a world of delights for us as Christian women. Read the following Scriptures and see for yourself.

John 10:10
"... I have come that they may have ______________, and have it ___________
_____________ _______________."

Ephesians 3: 16–21
"... to grasp how ___________, and ___________, and __________, and _____________ is the love of Christ ... that you may be ________________ to the ______________with the __________________ of God. Now to him who is able to do __________________ ________________ than all we ask or imagine, according to his power at work within us . . ."

Write the words to today's **Focus Verse** below and commit to memorize it before the next lesson.

____

____

What is God's desire for you?

As Christians, we know that God desires that we remain faithful and obedient to his Word. We know that he desires for us to be light and salt in a fallen world. But the details of how to accomplish his will are sometimes a bit fuzzy. In practical terms, how do I make sure that I am following his will for my life?

There was one in the New Testament who understood his calling.

Read John 3:22–30.

What complaint did John's disciples have? (v. 26)

In short, what was John's reply?

What was John the Baptist's purpose?

Could John have become bitter about Jesus' following and ministry?

____

Why didn't he?

____

John was not focused on himself. He knew that the One who was to come was greater than he and that his purpose was to point the way to Jesus.

Rick Warren in his book, "The Purpose Driven Life," says this: "Focusing on ourselves will never reveal our life's purpose."

The Apostle Paul said it first, "Everything got started in him and finds its purpose in him" (Colossians 1:16, Msg).

It is only when we seek first his kingdom and his righteousness and humbly surrender our lives to his power that we will begin to discover God's plan for our life.

I like how Max Lucado explains it in his book, *Let the Journey Continue: God's Roadmap for New Beginnings.* He asks the questions:

> What ignites your heart? Forgotten orphans? Untouched nations? The inner city? The outer limits? Heed the fire within! Do you have a passion to sing? Then sing! Are you stirred to manage? Then manage! Do you ache for the ill? Then treat them! Do you hurt for the lost? Then teach them!

God put within each of us certain desires and gifts to be used for his glory and purpose. Those things that get us excited, the things that beckon us are most likely the things we are supposed to do—for him.

I enjoy gardening. I love to be outside on a beautiful day with my headphones on and my hands in the dirt. That is a perfect day for me. I can hardly wait to get outside when the first not-so-cold days of spring come. My garden beckons me. Now, I haven't discovered yet how I might use that desire to fulfill a greater purpose. However, I also get excited about God's word. That too beckons me. I enjoy preparing to teach a Bible class or writing a Bible study for women. It is what I think about in the middle of the night. I become frustrated if too many days go by before I am able to get back to my study. God gave me the desire and gift to teach his word. It is something I must do.

Frederich Buechner said: "Calling is the place where your deep gladness meets the world's deep need." Isn't it amazing that God chooses to bless us with certain gladness in an activity or service that can also be used for the kingdom? That's all part of the abundant life he has planned for us! We will receive great joy and satisfaction by serving in the capacity we were designed for.

As we close our study today, consider the words of our **Focus Verse** again and begin to pray that God will guide you to discover the spark inside your heart.

Day 3

Opening the Gift

As we come to the end of this lesson, I hope that it is clear to you now that your life is part of a bigger picture. God has committed some work to you that he has not given to another. We are all parts of a whole in the kingdom of God, each one fulfilling her designated purpose, placing another piece of the puzzle. The end result—a world won for Christ!

Our focus today will be on opening that gift! Take a few moments to complete the survey below. It may seem awkward at first, but who knows you better than you? Honor God by answering as truthfully as you can.

What Are My Gifts?

Start by considering what special talents or skills you possess. What do you do well?

____

____

What do you like to do in your spare time?

____

____

Do you enjoy large gatherings or smaller events?

____

____

What have you done in the past that built up the church?

____

____

What age groups do you enjoy working with?

____

Is there someone in the church whose work you admire?

____

____

Is there something you've always dreamed of doing?

____

____

Now brainstorm ways you can use these skills to glorify God.

____

____

____

____

I'm sure that right about now you're feeling a little uncomfortable, afraid that you're about to commit to a lifelong ministry of some kind. Don't let your fear hold you back. Remember that you are just trying to identify what God's good and perfect will is for your life. He calls each of us to serve him in different ways. Maybe you have never quite discovered what that is for you. Take this opportunity for the Lord to guide you to that place of "gladness."

Now that you have the old brain warmed up and thinking, let's begin to think of a plan of action.

- Get together with a trusted sister and share your ideas with her.
- Ask her to pray with you about opportunities to use your gift(s).
- What preparation will you need? How can you grow in this area?
- Study?
- Practice?
- Training?
- Who do you know that could mentor you in your area of service?
- Are there scriptures that could help you focus on and support this purpose?

As you continue to follow the idea of developing your gifts, remember that those Bible characters that made the greatest impact on their world had assignments that were beyond their power and ability. God always works best with broken vessels. As long as you remain humble before God and surrender your will to his, he will enable you to accomplish far more than you could ever dream of!

Arthur Miller gave this description of "Seven-Days-a-Week Faith": "It is using one's endowed giftedness to serve the world with excellence and, through that service, to love and honor God! The calling that fully engages what God has given you is a holy task!"

May God bless you as you open your gift!

Dear Heavenly Father,

What a joy it is to be your child! I know that you are always watching over me and wanting good for my life. Help me to see the abundance that you have planned for me. Teach me to walk in your ways. Open my eyes to the blessings that you have hidden inside of trials. Like Joseph, may I always know that you have a plan for my life.

In the Name of Jesus,

Amen

For Additional Study

Read the entire book of Esther. It is not a long one. Her story so vividly describes what we have been talking about. Notice her humility and faith, even as a very young woman. See how she was willing to yield to the Lord's plan for her life. Pray that God will open your eyes to his dreams for you. Pray also for a willing and surrendered heart.

LESSON 3

Becoming:

How Can I Be Transformed into His Likeness?

> **FOCUS VERSE**
>
> Romans 12:2
>
> Do not conform any longer to the pattern of this world, but be transformed by the renewing of your mind. Then you will be able to test and approve what God's will is - his good, pleasing and perfect will.

Looking Back

I hope that you spent much time in prayer last week concerning God's plans for you. As we saw with the story of Joseph, God has a great plan for each of our lives. He desires that we fully submit to his leading in order to experience the abundance he promises. This week, we will begin thinking about how spiritual disciplines can help us to grow in our faith.

How is the Scripture memorization coming? I hope that you will look back frequently and review the **Focus Verses**. That is how we write them on our hearts. Jesus teaches in John 15 that his words are to remain in us so that we might remain in him. Be diligent about your Scripture memorization. You will truly see transformation!

Day 1

Basic Training

Isn't the word *transformation* an exciting one? All sorts of things fill my mind when I think of it: a fuzzy caterpillar going through all the necessary phases to become a beautiful butterfly, a lump of clay that is lovingly molded and shaped by an artisan's hands into a magnificent piece of pottery, or a young child as she changes into a beautiful young girl and then a mature woman. Webster defines transformation as "changing completely in appearance or nature."

What words come to your mind when you imagine one thing becoming another, completely changing in appearance or nature? Describe the experience.

____

____

Scripture clearly indicates that as Christians, God desires a spiritual transformation in each of us. We are called to live lives devoted to and reflective of Christ. One such example is found in Titus 2:11–14. What are the two teachings from the grace of God mentioned here?

____

____

____

There are activities that we are to say no to once we have put on Christ. We are instructed to live self-controlled, upright lives while we wait for the blessed hope—the appearing of our God and Savior.

What problem arises in us because of this teaching?

____

This type of disciplined lifestyle is totally against our nature. We are born with the inclination to live for ourselves. We come into this world with the attitude that it is all about us. Self-control is not a concept that we are eager to embrace as human beings.

Listen to these thoughts from Monroe Hawley, taken from his book, *The Focus of our Faith:*

> The faith of the average person has little focus. He views his religion as a group of unrelated actions structured around a moral code more determined by the values of society than the teachings of the Bible. Somehow it involves the idea of getting right with God and a hazy expectation of life after death, and is like a parachute in time of distress—try it when all else fails.

Spiritual transformation and the pursuit of holiness must become a priority if we are to fully realize who God intended us to be. If we aspire to be more than the average person mentioned above, we must set our minds on becoming transformed into the likeness of Christ.

The story's told of a little boy who fell out of bed. When his mother asked him how it happened, he replied, "I think I stayed too close to where I got in." Many Christians stay too close to the place where they "got in" spiritually. They never quite move out of the spiritual infancy.

It is a good idea for Christians to take stock periodically and ask themselves: "How do my spiritual habits today compare to what they were one year ago? Five years ago? When I first became a Christian?

How would you answer these questions?

Rate each spiritual habit: 3-very rewarding, 2-average, 1-a rare occurrence

	Bible Study	Prayer	Worship	Service	Joy
Today					
1 yr. ago					
New Christian					

Write 2 Corinthians 3:18.

____

____

____

Circle the words above that tell to what degree we are to be transformed. Draw a box around the words that tell from where this transformation comes.

Eugene Peterson in *The Message* describes this change as a sort of transfiguration-like experience. As we allow God to enter our lives and are changed by him, we become brighter and more beautiful.

You may say, "I am willing, but how do I get there? Do I just pray, read my Bible, and wait for 'the change?'" In his letter to young Timothy, the Apostle Paul spoke of "training in righteousness" (2 Timothy 3:16). What does that involve? We first need to know what righteousness entails. We learn that by studying God's word. Then we ask God to show us those characteristics within us that are weak or need to be practiced to a greater degree. Then, like the athlete, we set about practicing those skills which will bring us closer to our goal of becoming more like Christ. Spiritual growth is not about trying but about training.

How are these two concepts different?

____

____

____

Imagine a person who decides he wants to run a marathon. He knows it will be grueling, but he is determined to give it his best shot. He goes to bed early the night before, gets up, and has a light breakfast a few hours before the race and then heads out. He makes a decision to try very hard to run a marathon. Is that enough? Of course not! I'm sure you would agree that this is a laughable illustration. Without the proper instruction and training for months ahead of time, all the desire in the world will not accomplish the goal.

On the other hand, someone who decides to train for an athletic competition usually begins by assessing his weaknesses and concentrating on making those areas stronger. He sets goals and makes a plan for achieving them. My husband has been a teacher and coach for many years. We have two sons who have played many different sports growing up. I've been able to see firsthand the importance of daily practice sessions. A team doesn't just decide to show up on game day and play a game. They spend most of their time practicing for the game, working on those plays that will be used to win. I've also never heard either of my boys or my husband say how much they enjoyed the practice sessions. That part of the picture isn't very glamorous, and it usually requires some blood, a lot of sweat, and maybe even a few private tears. But it's necessary. You know the old saying: "Practice makes perfect."

The concept of training implies a steady, consistent effort, which in the spiritual sense also calls for prayer and dependence on God. Sometimes it feels like two steps forward, one step back. Keep in mind that when we dedicate ourselves to the pursuit of holiness, Satan tries all the more to take our focus off the goal.

Write the **Focus Verse** for this week on the lines below and commit to memorize it before the next lesson.

____

____

____

As we close our study today, pray that God will give you the desire for real transformation and that he will reveal those areas of your spiritual life which need to be reawakened. God wants to take you to new heights. Get ready!

Day 2

Spiritual Fitness

I hope that you are excited at the thought of what God is about to do in your life. We continue today to focus on putting ourselves in the position for God to do his work.

Once we have made the decision to become a Christian and have determined to allow God to change us from the inside out to be the women he designed us to be, the next step is to set our minds on the things of Christ. It is said that we become like the things we think about.

Transformation begins in our thoughts. The Roman philosopher Marcus Aurelius claimed that, "The soul is dyed the color of its thoughts."

Paul gives instruction on renewing our minds in his book to the Philippians in chapter 4, beginning in verse 8. List the things we are to think on.

____

____

____

____

How much of what society feeds us today falls into the "true, noble, right, and pure" category? Not very much!

Judging from this passage, what types of things are we not to think on?

____

____

I believe this Scripture also warns against negative thinking. Satan knows that spiritual growth cannot occur where there is negativity and doubt. I would imagine that Satan tried to have a hey-day with Paul's thoughts. I'm sure he tried to discourage Paul by planting seeds of doubt and guilt in Paul's mind. Paul could have spent the rest of his life regretting the persecution that he took part in during the early days of the church. He could have reasoned that there was no chance of him converting anyone to the cause of Christ with the life he had lived. I'm sure Satan reminded him often that he was lower than low for having been such a sinner. Instead, Paul accepted the grace God offered and said, "... forgetting what is behind and straining toward what is ahead, I press on toward the goal" Philippians 3:14.

Read what Paul had to say in his letter to the Corinthian Christians in 2 Corinthians 10:5.

"We demolish arguments and every pretension that sets itself up against the

knowledge of God, and we ____________________ ____________________ every

____________________ to make it obedient to Christ."

In order to renew our minds, we must be sure that our thoughts remain centered on truth. Satan will try to convince us that God could never use us for his purposes. Two of his greatest tools are discouragement and doubt. Remember sisters, he is a liar and the father of lies! God can and has used any individual who will humble herself in his sight.

The psalmist David knew how to renew his mind. He said it this way in Psalm 16:8: "I have set the Lord always before me. Because He is at my right hand, I will not be shaken." What a beautiful concept, to set the Lord before you continually; to practice being in his presence daily.

In what ways do you attempt to set the Lord before you?

____

____

____

Several years ago, I read a book entitled *Stepping Heavenward* by Elizabeth Prentiss. The book contained the journal of a young woman who determined to live her life in continual communication with God. She began her day with a conversation with the Lord and the conversation was ongoing all day long.

At the time that I read it, I had never thought of such a thing. It seemed such a lofty and admirable pursuit, but impossible to achieve. I tried to imagine my life in such an open communication with God that I spoke to him in my thoughts constantly throughout my busy day. At the time, I had two small boys and taught school. Though I tried to be the first in my house to awaken and spend a few moments reading my Bible, it seemed that once my day kicked into full speed there was never a quiet enough moment to pause and talk to the Lord. Now that I am an empty-nester most of the time (both boys are away at college) and no longer teach school, I am blessed to be able to spend a good deal more time focused on the Word and in prayer. Still, I would have to say that the "conversation" lags during the day. I tend to reserve the first hour of the day for quiet time, and then it's off to do the rest of my day.

Jesus refers to this type of centered living illustrated by the young woman in the story as remaining in Christ.

Read John 15:1–11.

Count the number of times he uses the phrase: "remain in me" or "remain in my love." ________________

What does it mean to remain in Christ?

____

____

What are the promises if we remain in him?

____

What does Jesus say are the consequences of not remaining in him?

____

____

____

I once heard an ancient proverb that said: "To attain knowledge, add things everyday. To attain wisdom, remove things everyday."

For us to see spiritual growth, it is essential to remain in Christ's teaching. This will provide the knowledge, motivation, and joy we need to continue to press on towards the goal.

Spiritual growth is a pursuit. It does not happen naturally or without effort. Just like the athlete who trains for a competition, we too must train our hearts and minds to be like Jesus. Our spiritual muscles, like our physical muscles, become weak and ineffective when they are not stretched and exercised regularly.

In the next portion of this lesson, we will talk about the habits that will help us to grow in our spiritual life. Start limbering up!

Day 3

Holy Habits

In his book *Set Apart: Discovering Personal Victory through Holiness,* Bruce Wilkinson coins the term "holy habits." He states that by changing your habits, you change your character.

Changing habits is a difficult thing to do. It has been said that it takes twenty-one consecutive days of practicing something for it to become a habit. It seems that it often takes at least that many days to change a habit as well. Adding a positive habit or breaking a negative one requires discipline.

Recently, I decided to renew my mind by finding more productive activities during the times that I might ordinarily sit down and watch television. I went on a TV fast for one week. Though difficult at first, it turned out to be a very rewarding experience. I had to retrain myself to find other things to do besides taking the path of least resistance. I found that most of the TV watching that I did was out of habit and not necessarily because I enjoyed the programs that much. During that week, I read more, did more of those little chores that I never seemed to have time for, and learned how to enjoy peace and quiet for a change. It also provided a quiet atmosphere to think. In today's hustle-and-bustle world, time to think is a rare commodity. Since that time, I have continued to watch far less television than before. It was a good experience for me, and it felt good to discipline myself away from a bad habit.

What are some good habits that we should practice?

____

____

In your own words, how would you define *discipline?*

____

____

____

The word discipline sometimes has a negative connotation. We often associate it with something that is unpleasant. However, I found six definitions for discipline in the dictionary, and only the last two related to punishment.

The first one listed was, "training, especially training of the mind or character."

Another was "to bring to a condition of order and obedience."

Both of these have very positive connotations. We have already mentioned that the Christian life is one of training in righteousness. Along with obedience to the laws of God, we are to train our minds to think like Jesus did. This is the renewal that our **Focus Verse** speaks of.

Norman Bales says, "Discipline is an avenue to holiness and holiness is the key to joy and peace."

Why does holiness require discipline?

____

____

How can a disciplined life lead to greater joy and peace?

____

____

____

____

King Solomon sets out his purpose in writing the book of Proverbs in the first few verses of chapter one. Read the first six verses.

What was his purpose?

____

____

Many, if not all, of the proverbs instruct us as to how to live a disciplined life. Let's look at just a few verses. Record briefly what each has to say about discipline.

Proverbs 1:7

____

3:11–12

____

5:22–23

____

12:1

____

13:18

____

13:24

____

15:32

____

19:18

____

Not only are we instructed to live ordered, disciplined lives ourselves, but we are also commanded to teach our children to live self-controlled lives. Without it we (and they) will come to ruin.

In what areas do you personally struggle with self-discipline?

____

____

____

My family is interested in fitness. My husband and both sons all work or study in the field of health and fitness. I have been a regular exerciser for years. We have become convinced that what you pay attention to improves. If you have the desire to improve your level of health, you can do so by practicing healthy habits.

The remaining lessons in this study will center around different spiritual habits that we can integrate into our daily lives to bring about spiritual growth. We will take the nine traits mentioned in Galatians 5:22–23, to base our habits on. In doing so, we will allow the Holy Spirit to transform our hearts and attitudes into the beautiful women God designed us to be before time began. We will discover how to truly become ourselves! I look forward to the next several weeks, and I'll be praying for you in your transformation process as well!

Dear Heavenly Father,

Thank you for seeing in me the potential to be a useful instrument in your kingdom. By your power, I will make a difference. Be ever before me throughout the day.

Whisper to me again and again of your loving care for the details of my life. Give me the self-control to say no to the world and yes to your promises.

Through Christ, my Savior,

Amen

For Additional Study

Continue to meditate on the **Focus Verses** you have learned, making personal application. Read the following Scriptures, and make note of those things we are to guard against and those things that we are to pursue for godliness.

1 Timothy 4:8

____

____

____

1 Timothy 6:11–21

____

____

____

2 Timothy 3

____

____

____

2 Peter 1:3–11

____

____

____

LESSON 4

What the World Needs Now:

Transforming Love

FOCUS VERSE

Galatians 5:22, 23

But the fruit of the Spirit is love, joy, peace, patience, kindness, goodness, faithfulness, gentleness and self-control.

Looking Back

You have completed three weeks of study. I hope at this point, you are finding yourself repeating those **Focus Verses** throughout the day. Let them bring focus to your heart as you continue on your path to becoming his. This week we will get down to the business of implementing certain habits that will help us grow in our spiritual lives.

Day 1

The Greatest Command

Write the **Focus Verse** for this week below, and commit to memorize it before the next lesson.

____

____

____

____

These Fruit of the Spirit help us to define our goals for transformation. They are the very characteristics that Jesus himself displayed and are the natural outgrowth of a life lived according to the Spirit. It's a tall order to be sure, but remember, we have the power that raised Jesus from the dead working within us!

We will begin with the first Fruit of the Spirit listed in Galatians 5:22: Love.

I suppose the Bible probably has more to say on the subject of love than on any other subject.

What scripture(s) come to your mind concerning love?

____

____

____

____

Let's begin our study by reading about love's beginning in 1 John 4:7–10.

What important truths do you see in this passage?

___

___

___

___

Read on in chapter 4. What does verse 16 say about how we know we are living in God and God is living in us?

___

Living a life of love is central to being a Christian. God is love! He holds his children to a high standard of love as well. We must continually challenge ourselves to grow in this area.

Let's read what Jesus had to say concerning love during his ministry.

Matthew 5:44

___

Matthew 19:19

___

Matthew 22:37

___

John 13:34

___

Is there anyone that we are not commanded to love? ____________
The apostles had much to say concerning love as well.
Romans 12:9 "Love must be ______________________________."
Romans 13:10 "Love is the _________________________ of the law."
1 Peter 4:8 "Love covers a multitude of _____________________."
1 John 3 18 "... let us not love with words or tongue but with
______________ and in ______________________."

Paul even goes so far as to say that, "The only thing that counts is faith expressing itself through love" (Galatians 5:6).

Fill in the chart below with some dos and don'ts concerning love. Use the scriptures listed for your answers.

Romans 13:10

1 Corinthians 8:1

1 Corinthians 13:4–7

LOVE IS/DOES	LOVE IS/DOES NOT

Why do you suppose there is so much teaching on love in the Bible?

____

____

Jesus said in John 15:13, "Greater love has no one than this, that he lay down his life for his friends." We know, of course, that one may literally give his life for a friend, but more often, we are called to lay down our lives in a spiritual sense. We may be asked to lay aside our hopes, dreams, and expectations on behalf of the rebellious teenager. We may be called to lay down our lives in forgiveness to the unfaithful spouse or the absent parent. Love may require that we lay down our lives in service to a cantankerous employer or a needy neighbor. Jesus said there is no greater expression of love than this. Selfless service and grace-filled giving were trademarks of Christ's life on this earth. They must be our ideals as well if we are to be transformed into his likeness.

Do these expressions of love always come easy? Explain.

____

____

____

Can you think of an example of this kind of extreme love in your own life or in the life of someone you have known?

What are the reasons that we often act in unloving ways toward others, even those we love?

____

____

____

I like the story of the little girl who came to her mother in tears. When asked what the problem was, she exclaimed, "I've been loving and loving all my little dollies, but they just won't love me back!" The little girl's frustration proves an important point. Love must be experienced.

How does one explain the love of a parent for a child to someone who has never had a child? Or the love of a husband for a wife to one who has never married? To tell someone you love him or her and not act in a way that would show that love is meaningless. It must not only be spoken but received in the form of loving touches, kind words, thoughtful acts, and selfless service.

In the next portion of this lesson, we will look at examples of love in action from God's word. Pray that the Lord will begin to soften your heart to all those around you and teach you to love like Christ.

Day 2

Love in Action

In today's study, we will look at two examples from Scripture of genuine love in action. One is from the Old Testament book of Hosea, showing the lengths to which God will go for his children. The second is from the New Testament, a story of human love born of forgiveness. As you study today, keep in mind that our goal is to have God transform our love lives and make us his chosen ambassadors in our world.

The book of Hosea is unique. It is an outstanding example of how creative God can be in getting our attention. During the period of history when God's people were divided into Israel in the north and Judah in the south, Hosea was commissioned to prophesy to idolatrous Israel. He was to warn them of the impending doom if they did not leave their pagan gods and return to the one true God. Hosea's personal life was to serve as a visual to the people of Israel of God's displeasure with them and his desire for their return to him.

Read Hosea 1:1–2.

What unusual request did God make of Hosea?

____

____

Why would God ask such a thing?

____

____

Continue reading in verses 3–8.

What was the name of Hosea's bride?

How many children did the couple have together?

___

How were the children's names chosen, and what was the purpose of their names?

___

___

___

In chapter 2, God speaks through Hosea to Israel concerning their unfaithfulness and the coming punishment. What is the metaphor that he uses?

___

In what way was Israel's unfaithfulness like that of an adulterous wife?

___

In chapter 3, we see the lengths to which God will go to bring his people back from their sin. Read all four verses.

Where does Hosea have to go to find Gomer?

___

What does Hosea give in exchange for his wife?

___

What might this transaction be alluding to?

___

After many pronouncements of judgment on the sinful nation, God declares his love for them once again. Look ahead to chapter 11.

To what does God liken the nation of Israel in this chapter?

___

The final verses of chapter 11 paint a tender picture of our loving God.

What does God say he will do for this "wayward child?"

___

___

___

This is a beautiful story of atonement and redemption. It illustrates the deep love of a Father for his child, even a rebellious one.

How does this story make you feel towards God?

___

___

The second part of our study today comes from Luke 7:36–49.

What is the occasion?

___

___

Describe the woman who comes to Jesus.

___

Why do you suppose that she begins weeping?

____

____

What extravagant show of love and appreciation does she display?

____

____

What did this act cost the woman?

____

____

How did Jesus contrast Simon's actions (or lack thereof) on Jesus' behalf with that of the woman?

____

____

____

What a beautiful story of love in action. The woman's love for Christ did not earn her forgiveness—it grew out of her forgiveness.

How much do you love Jesus?

____

____

In tomorrow's lesson, we will take a look at some specific habits that we can add to our lives in order to develop a more loving spirit. Be ready for action as we seek to grow!

Day 3

Holy Habits

Finally, we come to the practical part of our study on love. Knowing all that we do about the Bible's instruction concerning love is of no use unless we practice it.

How can we grow in this area? We have already read that we are to love our neighbor as we love ourselves. Herein lies the first important step: Learn to better love yourself. The concept of loving oneself seems awkward, doesn't it? However, as we can clearly see, it is the will of God.

Think back on those reasons why we act in unloving ways. We can not properly look after others if we haven't taken care of ourselves first. Haven't you heard the flight attendant explain that in case of emergency, parents should always put on their own oxygen masks first, and then help the child with his?

The Discipline of Rest

Could it be that the greatest thing we could do to be more loving to others is to get more rest? We see it so often in our young children; maybe we need to ask ourselves the question, "Do you need a nap, young lady?" Our schedules are often not conducive to a full eight hours of sleep every night. Our bodies are not able to function properly when we are sleep-deprived.

Physiologically, many things happen while we sleep. Several chemicals called neurotransmitters are released. These neurotransmitters are responsible for stimulating such activities as thinking, planning, and imagining. Consequently, we are not as sharp when we are sleep-deprived. It stands to reason that we would become short with those around us when we are in this kind of state. We are much more likely to say and do things we soon regret. How can we remedy this? Americans are not accustomed to afternoon breaks for resting as are some cultures. If your situation does not allow for this, why not make it a priority to get in bed one hour earlier? (It seems to work miracles for the little ones.) It will take a fair amount of self-discipline to look around at the chores that may not have been done and say goodnight anyway. Try it and see if your day isn't a little happier tomorrow.

The Discipline of Solitude

Another invaluable habit in learning to be more loving is to practice a period of solitude each day. Solitude means having a quiet time alone every day—no newspapers, music, or TV. It also means no husband or children for a time. You'd be surprised how difficult it is to just be alone and quiet. It will take a little practice. We are so unaccustomed to spending time alone with our thoughts that we seem to have forgotten how. The old adage, "silence is golden," means little to us today.

Consider the words to the rhyme below:

A wise old bird lived in an oak;

The more he saw, the less he spoke.

The less he spoke, the more he heard—

Why can't we all be like that bird?

Everyone needs some time every day to breathe deeply, plan for the day, or rehash the events of the day and prayerfully consider the work God has for us. We need to take time to "set the Lord before us" and seek the Lord's guidance every day. How often we see the example of Jesus retreating to a lonely place for time spent alone with his Father.

Listen to the wise words of Carolyn Savelle: "To spend little time with Jesus is to accomplish little in Jesus!"

There will always be the temptation not to take this time for you. Satan will make sure that it is never convenient to be alone with your thoughts. Whether you are raising small children or you live alone, something will always beg for your attention. The phone will ring, or you will think of something that needs to be done, or the dog will get out. If Satan can keep us from thinking about spiritual things, he knows that we will continue along the same path, never seeking to better our relationship with God or those around us. Once we learn to discipline ourselves to do this, we will find it easier to deal with others in a loving way.

Are you in the habit of spending quiet time alone every day?

During what time of day would this work best for you? Circle one.

early morning lunch time before bed

It does not have to be a long period of time. Even ten or fifteen minutes spent meditating on a scripture and saying a word of prayer will focus your thoughts for the day. There are also many good devotional books that have a prescribed short reading for each day. The point is that the time needs to be spent in a quiet, peaceful place and with the Lord. I challenge you to try this for one week consistently and see if it doesn't bring numerous blessings to you and to those around you.

As we close this lesson, let me encourage you to take your own inventory in the love department. Who in your life deserves a little extra TLC? Who in your life do you have difficulty loving? Maybe it's a coworker, a family member, or yourself. Consider trying one of the disciplines mentioned in today's lesson. Practice it throughout the coming week. Pray for strength—physically, mentally, and emotionally—to grow in love. Write out a plan below. You might want to confide in a good sister for some accountability.

____

____

____

Have a wonderful week serving the Lord!

My Loving Heavenly Father,

What a blessing to read of your love for me. How could I live without that knowledge? Show me, God, how to love others with that same unconditional love. Remind me of the grace you bestowed on me so that I will be grace-filled with those whom I come in contact. Help me to love myself and see myself as your precious daughter.

Through Christ I Pray,

Amen

For Additional Study

The apostle John learned much about growing in love during his lifetime. Remember the nickname given him early on in his discipleship? He and his brother James were called "Sons of Thunder" for their quick tempers and impatience. As an old man, however, John became an exile on the lonely island of Patmos. This is where he wrote the three short letters: 1, 2, and 3 John. Read through these brief letters. Listen for the wise words concerning love that he shares with you.

LESSON 5

The God Who Smiles:

Transforming Joy

FOCUS VERSE

Psalm 100

Shout for joy to the Lord, all the earth. Worship the Lord with gladness; come before him with joyful songs. Know that the Lord is God. It is he who made us, and we are his; we are his people and the sheep of his pasture.

Enter his gates with Thanksgiving and his courts with praise; give thanks to him and praise his name. For the Lord is good and his love endures forever; his faithfulness continues through all generations.

Looking Back

How is your love life? I'm not getting personal. I'm just wondering if you have seen progress in the area of loving others since our study last week. Paul taught in Romans 13 that love is the fulfillment of all the law. I encourage you to continue to pursue those activities that will help you in this endeavor of loving.

"Joy is the echo of God's life within us." What a beautiful description by Joseph Marmion. As we study today, we will see that, like love, the second fruit of the spirit, joy, comes straight from God.

Day 1

The Frosting on the Cake

Don't you like to be around people who are joy-filled? They just make you feel better. Sherwood Wirt, author of *Jesus, Man of Joy,* has some interesting thoughts on joy:

> What is joy? It is the enjoyment of God and the good things that come from the hand of God. If our new freedom in Christ is a piece of angel food cake, joy is the frosting. If the Bible gives us the wonderful words of life, joy supplies the music... (Joy) brings with it pleasure, gladness, and delight... It is more than fun; yet it has fun. It expresses itself with laughter and elation, yet it draws from a deep spring that keeps flowing long after the laughter has died and the tears have come.

God's word contains over five hundred references to joy. At least one hundred of these are found in the Psalms alone.

Write the words to our **Focus Verse** for this week below. Commit to memorize it before the next lesson.

This is a bit longer than our other memory exercises, but it's one you have probably read often and may already know. What a positive message it brings! It reveals to us the main reason we should have joy-filled lives: because we know that the Lord is God, and the Lord is good, and his love and faithfulness continue forever. God is the real joy giver!

On the lines below, write any words you can think of that relate to joy.

____

____

____

Just saying the words makes my heart lighter. How about you? Did you think of these: bliss, mirth, delight, exultation, merriment, satisfaction, fortunate?

I remember as a child learning the song, "I Have a Joy, Joy, Joy, Joy Down in My Heart." Children do have that bubbling joy, don't they? Why is it that we sometimes lose our joy as we grow older?

Let's look into the Scriptures and see what a few of those five hundred references say about joy. Match the verse to the message it gives about joy.

1. Deuteronomy 16:15	____ The prospect of the righteous is joy.
2. Nehemiah 8:10	____ The trees of the forest will sing for joy.
3. Psalm 96:12	____ Consider trials a pure joy.
4. Proverbs 10:1	____ The Lord will bless you and your joy will be complete.
5. Proverbs 10:28	____ Good news of great joy
6. Luke 2:10	____ The joy of the Lord is your strength.
7. Hebrews 12:2	____ Jesus, for the joy set before him endured the cross.
8. James 1:2	____ A wise son brings joy to his father.

These are but a fraction of the teachings about joy in God's word. Our prime objective in this lesson is to learn how we might have greater joy. However, I think it is important that we first see where God's joy lies. Let's look now at the messages of two of the Old Testament prophets about God's joy.

Turn to Zephaniah 3:17. This short book tells of God's judgment on the nation of Judah. The end of chapter 3 brings hope for the remnant of Israel. It tells of God's mercy and protection for those who follow him. Read verse 17 and tell where God's joy lies.

____

What will be his response to his people?

____

Now look at Isaiah 65. Read verses 17–25. What is this passage describing?

____

What does Isaiah say will be God's joy and delight?

____

Isn't it comforting to know that we serve a God who smiles? I love watching those programs on the nature channels about strange looking animals and insects. You know the ones where the camera looks eyeball to eyeball with the iguana? It always amazes me to see the brilliant colors, unusual shapes, and downright silly-looking animals that God created. Let's face it—God had to have enjoyed himself on that sixth day of creation. What fun it must have been designing all those unusual looking creatures. You just have to laugh when you look at those chimpanzees! Spend some time today rejoicing in the God who created laughter and joy. Go ahead, have a piece of that cake!

Day 2

Jesus, Man of Joy

God's desire for you and me is that we be filled with joy! I love the expression used by Sherwood Wirt. He talks about "living gladly." His book makes the point that Jesus must have lived a life full of joy. Yes, I know that the Bible describes him as a man of sorrows, but I believe, along with Mr. Wirt, that in order for people to have followed him as they did, he must have exuded a great deal of joy and peace. His message was certainly a positive one. People were drawn to him wherever he went. Children have an uncanny sense about people, and we know that the little children were often found enjoying the company of Jesus.

The cover of Wirt's book depicts a smiling Jesus. The scene is from *The Visual Bible: The Gospel of Matthew*. Bruce Marchiano, the actor portraying Jesus in the film, writes the forward to Wirt's book. In it, Marchiano tells that during the time of his work on *The Gospel of Matthew*, his understanding of the Savior completely changed. (This film had the same effect on me.) He went on to tell that he had come to the conclusion that society, as well as churches, have had an incomplete picture of the nature of Christ by not seeing that he truly was a man of joy. Wirt made the point in the book that if Jesus wept, he also laughed.

Joy is to be a natural part of the Christian's life—a fruit of the life lived in the Spirit. Does your life bring joy to God? Is he able to rejoice over you with singing? How about your friends and family? Are they uplifted and encouraged after spending time with you? Do you laugh a little every day? Are you able to find sheer delight in watching your children play or in looking at a sunset? Do you most often wear a smile or a pleasant expression or is it a worried, hurried, or angry look?

Think of someone in your life that seems to exude a joy-filled spirit.

____

What makes this person so joyful?

Have their circumstances always been happy ones?

Having a spirit of joy is not dependent on our circumstances. Some of the most joyful Christians have experienced a great deal of pain in their lives. With the help of the Holy Spirit, we can move beyond our pain to experience the deep joy of God.

Proverbs 15:13 says that a happy heart makes the face cheerful. Is your heart in need of a little more happiness? What in your life is keeping you from experiencing the joy God intends for you to have?

____

____

Write the words of Solomon from Ecclesiastes 3:12–13.

____

____

____

____

____

John Maxwell, author and motivational speaker, refers to two types of people: *lifters* and *leaners.* Another way to put it is *adders* and *subtracters.* Some of us lift people up and some of us weigh people down. We either add to the lives of those around us or we subtract from their lives. Which are you on most days?

What characteristics define these two types of people?

Lifters/Adders:

____

____

Leaners/Subtractors:

____

____

How would you categorize these Bible characters? Lifter or leaner?

Job's wife ___________________ Jonah ____________________

Pharisees ___________________ Daniel ___________________

Paul _______________________ Timothy ___________________

Nehemiah __________________ Ruth ______________________

We know that all good gifts (including joy) come from God, James 1:17. We can surely also agree that Satan is the ultimate joy-stealer. He uses many different tactics in his joy-sabotage scheme. Three main areas come to my mind:

Busyness

No one is busier than today's women. If Satan can convince us that we have more to do than we could ever get done, we will not allow ourselves the time to be joyful. Yes, joyfulness takes time.

Materialism/Debt

When we are always striving to make more money and get more stuff, we never feel content, which is one prerequisite of joy. The financial burden created by our "gotta have it" mentality enslaves us to our possessions. The Bible tells us it is impossible to serve God and money, Matthew 6:24.

Lack of Faith

Jesus, in the parable of the sower in Mark 4, tells us that one reason why the good news of the Gospel is choked out of the hearts of some is because of the worries of this life. What a tragedy to miss out on the greatest joy known to mankind because of the perceived magnitude of the troubles we face.

What are some other joy-stealers?

____

____

Satan is very crafty and often very effective in robbing us of the joy of being a child of God. We must constantly be on guard against his schemes.

Have you identified your greatest joy-stealer?

How can we train ourselves to be receptive to the joy God wants to bestow on our hearts? In the next part of this lesson, we will consider some holy habits that will help to increase our joy. In the meantime, take time out and smell the roses. Be blessed today!

Day 3

Holy Habits

In yesterday's lesson, we identified several joy-stealers in our lives. We concluded that one of Satan's most effective tools is discouragement and distraction. He would have us so preoccupied with the struggles of life that we miss the good things God sends us in the very ordinary activities of life.

A New Perspective

Robert Jeffress, in *The Road Most Traveled,* tells a story of three men who were all laboring at the same task. A pedestrian walked by and asked each one what he was doing. The first man answered, "I'm laying a stone." The second one replied, "I'm erecting a wall." The third man answered, "I'm building a cathedral." Each man saw his toil from a different perspective. Perhaps that is why some people find joy in their everyday tasks and others see them simply as chores that must be done. Maybe a change of perspective, a godly perspective, would serve to increase our joy level in the mundane things of life.

Ann Morrow Lindbergh observed, in her book, "Gift from the Sea," that most of us don't mind pouring our lives out for a reason. We do resent, however, feeling as though it is being dribbled away in small, meaningless drops for no good reason. We must begin to realize that all the activities of our life can be meaningful when dedicated to the glory of God. Our joy will increase when we start believing that the bits and pieces all add up in God's big plan.

Could you use a fresh perspective on your day-to-day activities?

____

How might you begin to experience more joy in the mundane-ness of life?

____

____

The Discipline of Contentment

Maybe your greatest joy-stealer has been falling prey to the temptation of materialism and debt. Being wrapped up in those credit card bills and juggling the paycheck every month to be sure all the creditors are satisfied makes it difficult to rejoice in the goodness of our God. It may mean that we need to fall on our knees before the Lord and confess the sins of greed and of poor stewardship of his blessings. We have to acknowledge the problem before we can begin working toward a solution. It may also be beneficial to embark on an extended study of Scripture in the area of contentment. Ask God to open your eyes to the true blessings in your life and to cause you to be disgusted with the media's attempts to create a constant craving for more. Monitor the amount of time you spend watching television or looking at written advertisements for material goods. These things affect us more than we realize when it comes to creating a feeling of discontent. Satan can gain a real stronghold on our lives by causing us to become discontent with what we have. It will take a great deal of commitment to change this dangerous habit and a prayerful heart to overcome it.

There are some wonderful books by Christian authors on managing your money and pleasing God in the area of stewardship. I can say from personal experience that the wise words from godly men such as Larry Burkett and Dave Ramsey helped to change my attitude towards money and things.

Would you be able to experience greater joy if you had a better understanding of money matters? What can you do to grow in this area?

____

____

Praying the Scriptures

Another valuable exercise for acquiring more joy is praying through the Scriptures. If you have never tried turning the promises of Scripture into prayers, you are in for a true blessing. It is a wonderful transforming experience when we begin to take the very words of God and claim them for our own. This might take a little practice at first, but it will surely help you to recognize God's faithfulness.

Choose a promise of Scripture such as 1 Chronicles 28:20, read the passage and rewrite it as a prayer. Below is an example of praying this Scripture.

Father, help me to be strong in your power and courageous to face my daily struggles. Keep me from fear and discouragement, for I know that you are with me. You will never fail me. You will never forsake me while I am serving you. In the Name of Jesus, Amen

Read the beautiful Psalm 46. Consider the truths and promises it relates. Reword a portion of the passage into a prayer.

___

___

___

___

___

___

___

Keep these written prayers in a journal and pray them often. Be sure and record the answered prayers! This will be a great faith builder as well as a joy bringer.

Our God is a God of joy! He wants nothing less for you and me. If you are in need of a little more joy in your life, I hope you will use some of these exercises in the days and weeks ahead. Life is hard. We need to be proactive in keeping that light of joy in our hearts. Be consistent about your training. You will reap great rewards! Have a great week in study and service to God and don't forget to celebrate!

Dear Heavenly Father,

I have a joy deep in my heart that comes only from being your daughter. I thank you for the beautiful gift of your love. Help me each day to see all around me the special little treasures created just for me. Open my eyes to the beauty in each individual I meet. May I be your instrument of beauty and joy to all those around me.

Through the blessed name of Jesus,

Amen

For Additional Study

There are some wonderful hymns of praise, some old and some more recent, that are great heart-lifters. I think God knew that singing would be important for us as part of our worship and a great encouragement for his people. Try to obtain a copy of the following hymns either online or in a borrowed hymnal and meditate on their words. Many are based on actual scriptures. Be encouraged!

"Joyful, Joyful We Adore Thee"

By Henry van Dyke and Ludwig van Beethoven

"Jesus, Name Above All Names"

By Naida Hearn

"Fairest Lord Jesus"

By Richard S. Willis

"Boundless Love"

By Dennis Loewen

LESSON 6

Sleeping Like a Baby:

Transforming Peace

FOCUS VERSE

Proverbs 3:5, 6

Trust in the Lord with all your heart, and lean not on your own understanding; in all your ways acknowledge him, and he will make your paths straight.

Looking Back

I hope that you have spent the past week with a deeper awareness of the blessings in your life and have noticed a true lightening of your spirit. Have you identified the joy-stealers in your life and begun some new spiritual habits to help increase your joy? Keep plugging away! Discipline always pays off!

This week, we will turn our attention to the blessing of peace. It truly is a blessing to the children of God and an attribute that we are instructed to pursue daily.

Day 1

Conflict Resolution

Do you think that peace is something most people experience on a regular basis? How do you know?

____

Truth be told, most people would probably confess that their lives are not very peaceful. Peace is a foreign concept to many, I'm afraid.

The words of an old hymn by John Greenleaf Whittier express perfectly what should be our prayer: "Take from our lives the strain and stress, and let our ordered lives confess the beauties of thy peace."

I suppose peace could be described as the absence of conflict. Until we reach heaven, we will not know a life absent of all conflict. We are all aware of the lack of peace within and between nations of the world. More importantly, however, is learning to find peace within ourselves that will sustain even through times of outward conflict.

In the 1970s, two noted psychologists named Holmes and Rahe developed a stress test that assigned a point value to the various life changes that cause us to be stressed or experience anxiety. They referred to these as stress units. Below are a few of the many situations that they came up with.

Taken from Stress Chart developed by Holmes and Rahe

Death of a spouse	100 units
Divorce	73
Death of close family member	63
Personal injury or illness	63
Marriage	50
Retirement	45
Pregnancy	40
Mortgage or loan over $10,000	31
Son or daughter leaves home	29
Change in residence	20
Vacation	13
Christmas	12

Researchers have determined that the accumulation of two hundred or more stress units in a single year is usually followed by significant increase in physical or psychiatric disorders. Millions of dollars are spent each year on medications to counter the effects of stress and anxiety. According to the American Academy of Family Physicians, two-thirds of office visits to family doctors are the result of stress-related symptoms. Research has shown that stress can be a contributing factor, either directly or indirectly, to heart disease, lung ailments, cirrhosis of the liver, and suicide. Peace seems to elude us in today's frantic society. The Bible has much to say concerning peace.

Take a look at these words to the nation of Israel regarding peace.

Numbers 6:22–26: What was the occasion or reason for these words?

____

Deuteronomy 7:9: To what extent will God keep his promises?

____

Psalm 9:10: How can we know that God is trustworthy?

____

____

Psalm 119:165: What promise is there for those who love the law of God?

____

Jesus himself had much to say regarding the topic of peace in his Sermon on the Mount. Let's look at Matthew 6:25–34.

Isn't it amazing that even thousands of years ago, Jesus knew the kinds of worries that we would struggle with in the twenty-first century? Things haven't really changed much, have they?

What kinds of things does Jesus tell us not to worry about?

____

He begins by telling his listeners not to worry about their lives. He then mentions food and clothing. In verse 27, he alludes to worries about health. Lastly, he says not to worry about the future.

What does Jesus tell his followers to spend their energy on?

____

What do you think he meant?

____

____

How would this bring peace?

____

____

____

The **Focus Verse** for this week gives the key to having a peaceful heart. Write the words from Proverbs 3:5–6 below. Commit to memorize them before the next lesson.

____

____

____

____

I'll close this portion of our lesson with a story that Gordon MacDonald, author of *Ordering Your Private World,* tells about a friend who was an officer aboard a U.S. Navy nuclear submarine. On one occasion, while on duty in the Mediterranean, there were many ships overhead on the surface. The submarine had to make several strategic maneuvers to avoid collisions. MacDonald's friend was the officer in charge of giving the commands as to where the submarine was positioned. Because of the frequent, unusual movements, the captain decided to go to the bridge to see if everything was all right. The commanding officer replied, "Yes, sir!" The captain took a quick look around and then turned to leave. "It looks all right to me too," he said.

This encounter between a naval officer and his trusted commander provides a valid picture of the peace of mind that can exist when the core being is in order. Although potential danger loomed in the waters overhead, deep inside, things were calmly controlled by highly trained seamen. Because of the many occasions when the procedures were practiced, when it came time for an actual encounter, there was no need for panic.

As Jesus reminded us in his sermon, we are of immeasurable worth in God's eyes. He knows what we need. He is capable of caring for all of the birds of the air and the wildflowers of the fields. How much more will he take care of his beloved children's needs! In the next section, we will remember together a faithful believer who trusted God with his very life. Come ready to be challenged!

Day 2

Beyond Understanding

We continue in our study of peace today. Before spending most of our time in the Old Testament, let's first look at three important lessons from the New Testament.

Read John 16:33: What are two certainties we see in this verse of Scripture?

___

Read Romans 5:1: What prerequisite is given in this verse to having peace with God?

___

Read Philippians 4:6–7: What two commands are given? What will be the result?

___

___

___

It is a fact that without God, we would have no peace in this life. Jesus came to be our Prince of Peace.

There is no greater example of God's peace in troubled times than that seen in the Old Testament character, Daniel. He was only a young man, possibly still a teen, when King Nebuchadnezzar of Babylon captured Judah and took many of its people as slaves. (That could cause a person's stress units to number into the triple digits!) Because of his academic skills and social graces, Daniel was chosen to train for service to the king.

Read Daniel 1 and notice Daniel's single-minded purpose.

He resolved to remain faithful to his God and not defile himself with the unclean practices used in preparing the king's food or from drinking wine in the king's house. God honored Daniel's faithfulness, and he and his friends all proved to be healthier and better nourished at the end of the trial period.

How did God further show favor to Daniel and his friends?

____

Daniel's amazing story continues in chapter 2. Because of the skill and understanding that God had bestowed on him, Daniel was given the opportunity to interpret the king's dream. When the king's men were unable to tell the king what he dreamed, they were ordered executed. Rather than to stand by and watch the men be killed, Daniel went to the king and asked for an opportunity to help.

Read verses 16–19 in chapter 2.

Where did Daniel go when he left the king?

What did he request?

____

He was confident in the God he served and immediately turned over his problems to him. Notice the humility in Daniel's prayer (verses 20–23).

After seeking God's guidance and wisdom on the matter, Daniel returned to the king and was able not only to interpret the dream but to describe the dream as well.

What was the result of Daniel's faithfulness? (Verses 47–49.)

____

____

____

The story most familiar to us in Daniel's life was that of the night spent in the lion's den. Chapter 6 tells of the trap set by the king's administrators. Because Daniel refused to bow down and worship any god other than the true and living God, he was thrown into the den of lions. When the king came to inquire of Daniel, he was surprised to hear Daniel's strong voice from the pit.

What was Daniel's answer in verse 21?

____

____

King Darius, after finding Daniel unharmed, had much the same response as King Nebuchadnezzar in chapter 2. Read his decree in verses 25–27.

Throughout Daniel's life, we see evidence of a confidence and peace that permeated his being. We know that his confidence was not in his own power but in that of the Almighty God he served.

What can give us that kind of faith in God that allows us to sleep peacefully at night? It was Daniel who recognized God's sovereignty in Daniel 4:25 when he told the king that God gave the kingdoms of the world to whomever he wished.

What does it mean that God is sovereign?

Author and speaker Chuck Swindoll defines it this way: "Our all-wise, all-knowing God reigns in realms beyond our comprehension to bring about a plan beyond our ability to alter, hinder, or stop."

That simply means that God is in control! We don't have to worry about ________________ (you fill in the blank). We can sleep peacefully at night, knowing that God has a plan for our lives and he will work it out. Does that mean that we are helpless puppets in the game of life? No! God gives each of us the right to choose between right and wrong and to choose the path we follow. (That's how Nebuchadnezzar ended up in his predicament.) It's a difficult concept to sort out, but I know that God is not bound by our free will choices. He will accomplish his plans through us or in spite of us. That brings tremendous peace and comfort to the Christian.

In the last section of our lesson, we will examine some ways that we can grow in this area of peace. God intended for his children to sleep well each night. Remember, he stays up all night so that we don't have to.

Day 3

Holy Habits

Now that we know that God desires for all of his children to rest in his peace, how can we better pursue that trusting, relaxed mindset?

What keeps us from trusting in God's sovereignty?

____

____

Most people who would call themselves believers spend less than two minutes each day in prayer, not counting at meals or in church. If you don't count church-related Bible study, most believers spend less than three minutes per day in God's word. Is it any surprise that we don't have a sense of fellowship and peace with God with those kinds of spiritual habits?

The Discipline of Morning Prayers

A regular time of morning prayer and meditation on God's Word will place us in the proper mindset to meet each day's trials. If we have already confessed our inability to maneuver through the day's stresses alone and we have asked the Lord to be at our side through specific activities facing us that day, we will not be tempted to rely on our own strength. We will feel empowered by the Holy Spirit to calmly approach each activity or individual, knowing that we are not alone. This prayer time is best done in the morning before the activities of the day begin to overwhelm us. We can start out with a sense of God-confidence and awareness that we are not alone.

A good friend recently shared with me a handmade card that I taped to my bathroom mirror to remind me of this practice. It says: "Good Morning, This is God. I'll be handling your problems today, and I do not need your help. Have a great day!" You'd be surprised how effective that little message is, and I love the dear friend who took the time to make it for me!

Do you currently set aside time each morning for prayer?

How might this practice enhance your sense of peace throughout the day?

____

____

What or who might you specifically pray about before beginning your day?

____

____

Practicing God's Presence

I like the phrase I've been hearing lately: "Practicing the presence of God." What a concept—that we would need to practice being aware of God's omnipresence. You may say, "How can I practice God's presence? He is with me whether I am aware of it or not." Cultivating the habit of being aware of God's constant presence and care for us is for our benefit, not God's. God has promised over and over to be with us always, but the cares of the world and Satan's ongoing attacks cause us to forget that the God of the universe stands by our side, ready to strengthen and guide us in every situation.

When we can begin to experience God on a daily basis, we will be able to worship him seven days a week, not just in a group setting on Sundays. As a matter of fact, our most sincere worship experiences will occur when we can identify his hand in our lives Monday through Saturday. Praise and adoration for his divine leading, answered prayers, and abiding peace will soon pour forth from hearts that are tied to his continually.

It may seem a bit forced at first, but keep working at it. Talk to the Lord in brief interchanges throughout the day. Work on memorizing a scripture whenever you are waiting on a traffic light or holding on the telephone. Tune your radio to a Christian station and listen to uplifting music or a message from the scriptures. Pretty soon you'll find your mind set on things above more than you realize.

What can you do to be more aware of God's presence daily?

____

As we close this lesson, I challenge each woman reading this to make a conscious effort to include God in every activity of the coming week. Each time you hear the shrill sound of a siren, pause and say a quick prayer for those who may be in harm's way. Whenever you pass a stranger in the grocery store or at the bank, quickly ask God's blessing on them. As you go through your morning routine, ask God to be a part of the day's activities and thank him for the strength he provides. Post a comforting scripture over your kitchen sink or on your desk at work. Become more aware of his presence, and relax in the knowledge that he truly does "have the whole world in his hands."

Dear Father in heaven,

Thank you for peaceful sleep and for your angels that encamp around me. You deliver me and keep me safe. Father, I thank you that even while I sleep, my heart counsels me and reveals to me your purpose and your plan. My heart is glad and my spirit rejoices; my body and soul rests confidently in your safety.

Through my loving Savior, I pray,

Amen

For Additional Study

Read each of the following Scriptures and record the promise.

Matthew 6:25–34

____

Matthew 4:19

____

Luke 12:6, 7

____

Isaiah 26:3

____

Read Psalm 104 and write a short statement describing it below.

____

____

____

____

LESSON 7

Ladies in Waiting:

Transforming Patience

FOCUS VERSE

Ephesians 4:2

Be completely humble and gentle; be patient,

bearing with one another in love.

Looking Back

How have you been sleeping? I hope you have noticed a more peaceful heart since our study last week. Have you made a point to set aside time each morning to begin your day with prayer? God is so eager to bestow on you his abiding peace.

This week, we move on in our pursuit of transformation with a look at patience. Someone has said, "Patience is the ability to count down before you blast off." That's a good definition, don't you think? What causes us to become impatient with others, ourselves, or even with God? We'll explore these questions in detail in this week's lesson. Be prepared for some hard work. This one really goes against the grain. With the power of Christ, however, we'll be able to see transformation in this area of our lives as well.

Day 1

It's About Time

The Quaker missionary Thomas Kelly once said, "People nowadays take time far more seriously than eternity." Kelly died in 1941. How much more true are his words today? We live in a society that seldom has to wait for anything. We've become accustomed to instant meals, thanks to microwave ovens and drive-thru windows. We can access information of any sort in a matter of seconds with our high-speed Internet. The least amount of time spent waiting for anything these days has us in a tizzy. Even with all our modern conveniences, we have so little time. This type of lifestyle seems to bring out the worst in us as we snap at those who slow us down.

The Greek origin of the word patience implies both forbearance and endurance. To forbear is to hold back—to keep from doing something. We will consider this aspect of patience regarding our relationships with other people. Endurance, on the other hand, refers to holding out, bearing up, or withstanding. We will look at this aspect of patience as it relates to our ability to wait on God.

What kinds of things cause you to become impatient?

____

____

There are many verses of Scripture we could have selected for our **Focus Verse** this week; however, Ephesians 4:2 contains two additional traits relating to patience that I don't want you to miss.

Write the scripture below and commit to memorize it before the next lesson.

____

____

____

What two traits does the apostle Paul mention in the above Scripture along with patience?

______________________________ and ______________________________

Is it possible to possess a patient spirit toward others without humility? Why or why not?

____

____

____

How does gentleness play a part in being patient?

____

____

____

Bearing with Others

Mac McCleary said, "Patience is something you admire in the driver behind you and scorn in the one ahead."

We all want to be shown patience, but how difficult it is to forbear with others! We often fall back into that mindset, "It's all about me."

Jesus calls us to stick and stay with those we love. This is not an easy thing sometimes. Patience is not something we are born with. If you don't believe that, you have never had the responsibility of caring for an infant. A newborn expects to have his every need met immediately. If not, he will cry until it is met. It takes many years of training for a child to learn that the world doesn't revolve around him. (Some take much longer to learn this than others!)

There are many verses in the New Testament which teach us how we are to interact with one another. Read each of the following and make a note of the commands you see.

Romans 12:10: "Be __________________________ to one another

__________________________ one another above yourselves."

Romans 14:19: "Do what leads to ____________________________ and ____________________ ________________________________."

Ephesians 4:32: "Be ___________________and ____________________________ to one another, __________________________ each other."

Hebrews 3:13: "________________________________one another daily."

Hebrews 10:24: "__________________ one another on toward _____________ and good deeds."

Patient Listening

One of the most important aspects in being patient with others is listening. If we can learn to practice the art of really listening to people, we will avoid many conflicts and enjoy more rewarding relationships. Everyone has a deep need to be heard. We all want to know that someone has listened to what we have to say and considered our views important. Too often we think we know what the other person's intentions or thoughts are, and we neglect to give them opportunity to explain themselves. Have you ever known someone who was constantly finishing your sentences for you? (I must confess I have been that person, especially with my husband.) This is a sign of impatience and, to a certain degree, arrogance. Remember, as our **Focus Verse** says, patience involves humility. Listening to another is an expression of a humble spirit.

Who do you know that is an exceptional listener?

Choice Words

Another facet of bearing with others is learning to hold our tongue. In the very familiar thirteenth chapter of 1 Corinthians, Paul explains that to be patient and kind toward others is to show them the love of Christ. It is not necessary that we say everything that comes to our minds. Learning to refrain from verbalizing our every thought and refusing to criticize others are signs of spiritual maturity.

James writes that the tongue is like a fire, capable of destroying. He also calls it a restless evil, full of deadly poison, unable to be tamed. That tells us that it takes constant vigilance to monitor and control our words. So much harm can be done with a careless tongue, yet so much good is accomplished with patient and thoughtful words.

Could your words use a little polishing? How might you change your speech in order to show patience?

____

____

As we close today's study, remember our **Focus Verse** for the week. Patience requires humility and gentleness. Listening carefully to others and guarding our lips are expressions of a humble spirit. In the next portion of this lesson, we will consider how to grow in our ability to wait on God.

Day 2

Holding Out

As difficult as it is to show patience with those around us, it is even more challenging to have patience with the Lord. Enduring, holding out, and bearing up under trying circumstances while waiting for God to act on our behalf is extremely difficult. Lewis Smedes, renowned Christian author and theologian said: "Waiting is the hardest work of hope."

The truth is that growth takes place in the waiting.

Darryl Rosen recently wrote a book called, *Surviving the Middle Miles: 26.2 Ways to Cross the Finish Line with Your Customers.* Though the book is written to inspire businessmen and women, I believe it has a lesson for us as well. Rosen, an avid runner since he was thirteen years old, tells of a time when he decided to try to qualify for the Boston Marathon. He explains that for some odd reason, though he knew better, he started the race as if he was running a hundred-yard dash. It wasn't long into the race when he began struggling. As it turned out, he never made it to the finish line. His book is about the race of life. In it, he says, "The real race begins in the middle miles." We often start a new thing with enthusiasm, but holding out when things get tough is when the real race begins.

So it is with our spiritual lives. God's will for our lives doesn't always move in a straight line. He is not bound by time and doesn't always follow the schedule we have in mind. Over and over in God's word we are instructed to "wait on the Lord."

There are many references to this type of waiting in the Bible. Let's consider God's servant Abraham first.

What a trusting and patient man Abraham must have been. We know from the twelfth chapter of Genesis that God called Abram (later to be known as Abraham) to leave his homeland and his father's household to move to a place that he would show him. The command came with great promises to Abram and his family; nevertheless, Abram was not informed as to where he was to relocate. Read the account in Genesis 12:1–9.

We are not given any indication that Abraham questioned God concerning this journey. He simply "left, as the Lord had told him," traveling from Ur to the land of Canaan. This distance would have been over two thousand miles. What patience it must have taken on behalf of Abraham and Sarah as they traveled day after day, year after year, waiting for the Lord to tell them that they had arrived at their destination!

Along with the promise of a new homeland, Abraham and Sarah were also promised a son. We know that they waited many years for the fulfillment of this promise since Ishmael, the son of Sarah's handmaid, was about fourteen at the time of Isaac's birth. (Ishmael and Isaac both suffered because of Sarah's failure to wait on God in that situation.) The complete account is found in Genesis 15–18.

In the story of Abraham and Sarah, we are reminded that God's timing and ours are not always the same.

Isaiah 55:8–9:

"For my ________________ are not your ________________, neither are my ________________ your ________________ declares the Lord. As the heavens are higher than the earth, so are my ________________ higher than your ________________ and my ________________ than your________________."

Remember Jairus, the synagogue ruler whose only daughter was dying? Read their story in Luke 8:40–56.

What happened as Jesus was on his way to Jairus' house?

____

____

After the woman was healed and Jesus continued on his way, a servant from Jairus's house met them. What did he say?

____

____

What was Jesus' response?

____

How did the girl's parents react to the resurrection?

____

Could it be that more good was accomplished, and God was glorified because of the wait?

You'll remember that the Israelites were made to wander in the wilderness for forty years before reaching Canaan, when the actual travel time would have been about eleven days. Once again, God's ways are not our ways.

Read Deuteronomy 8:2–4.

Why did Moses say that God had led them for forty years?

____

____

____

Often God allows us to go through a period of waiting or testing before he enters our situation. It is during these times that we must remain faithful in prayer and constant in the Word. God is never late, and he always knows what's best for us. As in the case of Mary, Martha, and Lazarus in John 11, God sometimes allows us to wait on him so that his glory may be revealed. Lazarus had been in the tomb for four days before Jesus finally arrived? Jesus did not show up when Mary and Martha had hoped, but because God knew best they were able to see even greater power displayed. Although we may not see him, our Father is there even during those middle miles.

Write Isaiah 40:31.

____

____

____

____

What is it that you are currently waiting for God to do in your life?

____

____

____

____

Have faith. Know that God hears your prayers and he loves you very much. His ways are not our ways, but praise God; his ways are so much higher! Trust that God is working out his divine plan for you.

Tomorrow's lesson will be the practical work. How can we learn to cultivate patience? You'll have to *wait* and see!

Day 3

Holy Habits

Patience is a virtue that can be cultivated. Just like the other fruit of the spirit, with a little discipline and determination, we can learn to be better waiters.

The Practice of Slowing

Try this! John Ortberg, in his book *The Life You've Always Wanted,* speaks of an exercise called *slowing.* Here is how he describes it: "This involves cultivating patience by deliberately choosing to place ourselves in positions where we simply have to wait. (This practice has a definite "game-like" quality, although we may not like it much, at least at first.)"

He goes on further to give suggestions for this little game.

- Try driving in the slow lane for a week. (No honking allowed!)
- How about deliberately choosing the longest check-out line at the grocery store. (Better yet, let one person go ahead of you.)
- Consciously chew each bite of food twenty-one times before swallowing.
- Leave your watch at home.

These may sound like silly ideas, but the point is to learn to live more slowly. We live such fast-paced lives these days. This type of "go, go, go" lifestyle is not conducive to holiness. If we didn't always feel rushed in our daily activities, we might just enjoy the wait. I'm convinced we miss all kinds of blessings because we are too busy to notice or enjoy them. A phrase I like is "live intentionally." Slow the pace of your life in order to make intentional, deliberate choices about how you will respond to people. Ask God to help you accomplish what you need to each day and trust that he will do it! (Oh, and you may need to leave the house a little earlier!)

In what area of your life do you need to slow down and live intentionally?

____

____

Controlled Breathing

It is a fact that slow, controlled breaths will lower blood pressure and anxiety.

Many of the stress-management books that are on the shelves today prescribe deep breathing and other forms of bio-feedback to lessen stress. This is a safe, relaxing way to decompress and clear your head. Practice inhaling deeply from the diaphragm. (When done correctly, your stomach will rise, not your chest.) Try to draw the breath over a period of three to five seconds, then slowly release it. With practice, I'm told it is possible to work up to ten to fifteen seconds. This could be a useful tool when dealing with difficult coworkers, handling delays, or just providing a nice break during a hectic day. You'll be surprised how much more clearly you will be able to think and act.

At what time of day or during what situations might controlled breathing benefit you?

____

____

Positive Self-Talk

An exercise sure to change your attitude and help with learning patience is to consider your self-talk. We all do it; we talk ourselves into and out of things every day. With positive self-talk, we can calm our spirits and relieve stress. Negative self-talk serves only to agitate our spirits and make us feel worse. Here are a few exercises to try:

1. Become aware of your patterns. Be conscious of your inner dialogue.

2. As you notice yourself beginning to grow impatient, say "Stop!" This will cause you to reevaluate the situation and think more clearly.

3. Adapt your statements with milder words. Instead of "I hate traffic! It makes me angry!" say: "I don't like traffic. It makes me annoyed."

The biblical command to "take captive every thought" will slow you down and cause you to see things from a new perspective.

What kind of things could you say to yourself when you start to feel impatient?

____

____

As we close this lesson, I urge you to work diligently in the coming week on practicing the discipline of patience. You will rarely regret your actions or words when you have taken the time to carefully think about your response to others ahead of time. Wait patiently on the Lord as he moves in the circumstances of your life. Be patient with yourself, trusting that God, who began a good work in you and will carry it on to completion until the day of Christ Jesus.

With whom or in what situation will you pledge to practice this attribute in the coming week?

____

Take it easy and have a great week!

Dear Lord God in heaven,

Thank you for your enduring patience with me. How I must try you at times! Forgive me for my impatience with those around me. I need your strength and your Spirit to teach me to be humble and consider others more important than myself. Help me to learn to wait on you, Lord. Your ways are so much higher than my ways! Calm my anxious heart, and remind me that you are in control. Bless me with your perfect peace.

In Christ's precious name,

Amen

For Additional Study

"It is a mistake to look too far ahead. Only one link in the chain of destiny can be handled at a time." Winston Churchill

As we consider living patiently, read the following verses relating to quietness. Make a note of the benefit or blessing in quietness.

Psalm 23: 1–2

____

____

Zephaniah 3:17

____

____

1 Timothy 2:1–2

____

____

1 Peter 3:3–4

____

____

Isaiah 30:15

____

____

LESSON 8

Living a You-First Life in a Me-First World:

Transforming Kindness

FOCUS VERSE

Proverbs 12:25

An anxious heart weighs a man down,
but a kind word cheers him up.

Looking Back

As we come to our eighth week of study together, I hope that you are realizing transformation in your life. God alone can work such amazing wonders in our hearts. He does require of us a willing and diligent spirit, committed to meditation on his word, honest prayer, and focused training on better habits. At this point in our study, you should have seven new scriptures committed to memory from which you can draw strength and encouragement in your journey. Press on! We enter a new topic this week which, when practiced, will serve to increase your joy, help you practice patience, and show the Father's love all at the same time!

Day 1

The Kind Ones

Fill in the blanks below.

Galatians 5:22–23
"The fruit of the spirit is ______________________, ____________________,
__________________________, ___________________________,
__________________________"

Today we begin looking at the fruit of kindness.

Finish the statement below.

Kind people …

____

____

Have you noticed that our society has come to tolerate rudeness? It doesn't even surprise us anymore when people don't speak or acknowledge one another in passing. Somewhere along the line, we have become a people who, whether to save time or keep from getting involved, seem to move through our day focused on the task at hand and guarded from personal interaction with others. Kindness has become, sadly, the exception more often than the rule.

So what does it mean to show kindness? Is it just a matter of being polite or does it require more? What does it mean when the Bible speaks of showing kindness to others?

Let's begin by looking at the Apostle Paul's words to the Ephesians.

Read Ephesians 5:1–2. Tell why we are commanded to show loving kindness to others.

____

____

If we are to look like our Father in heaven, we must exhibit the loving nature of the Father and of Christ Jesus. We have a wonderful example to follow in Christ. There can be no greater kindness than that of Jesus giving his own life for us. Paul said this was a fragrant offering and sacrifice to God (Romans 12:1). We are called to be that kind of living sacrifice as well.

A kind person cares about other people. Have you known someone who just seemed to have a real sense of compassion for the needs of others? They always seem to be the first to the side of the one who is grieving or lonely. They never have to be asked to offer assistance—they just know and they just act. This is kindness.

Christians in the first century were often called "the kind ones." This may have been due, in part, to the fact that the word for Christ, *Christos,* and the word for kindness, *chrestos,* were very similar. Hopefully it had more to do with the kind actions of the Christ followers.

True kindness is prompted by humility. We will not take the time and effort to show kindness to another unless we can first see their needs as more important than our own at any given time. The mindset of servant-hood is crucial to this type of unselfish living.

You may remember a major motion picture from several years ago called *Pay It Forward.* In the film, Haley Joel Osment portrays an eleven-year-old boy, Trevor, who is given an assignment in his history class to come up with an idea that would change the world. His idea was for each person who experienced a kind act done by another to pay it forward (rather than pay it back) by showing three other people an act of kindness. Those three would, in turn, each choose three people to show kindness, etc. Trevor's idea, if implemented in real life, would indeed change our world, wouldn't it?

Let's look at a biblical example of a kindness done to an individual whose life depended on the kindness of others. During the reign of King David, at a time when the Lord was giving David great victories wherever he went, David remembered his predecessor, King Saul. Saul's son and David's dear friend, Jonathon, was dead, and David wanted to do something for one of Saul's household. Let's begin by going back to a time when David and Jonathon made a covenant with each other. You remember that Saul was angry with David because the Lord had found favor with him. David was in hiding, and Jonathon was to speak to his father and get a sense of what his plans were concerning David.

Read 1 Samuel 20:11–17.

What was the request Jonathon made of David in the field?

Now turn and read 2 Samuel 9 to see the fulfillment of the promise by David.

Who of Saul's household was still living?

What disability did the young man have?

What did David do for Jonathon's son?

Notice the last part of verse 13. We are reminded again that Mephibosheth was crippled in both feet. What sort of people do you think were usually invited to sit at the king's table? How often do you suppose that the lame or the destitute were invited? I would imagine that it was a rare occurrence.

Whose kindness did David wish to show, according to verse 3?

Turn to 1 Peter 4:8–10.

What does Peter say we do when we serve others?

We become the hands and feet of God when we show loving kindness to others.

How great is that! If you want to do the work of God on earth, get out there and show his grace to those who need it. (There's no one who doesn't need it!) The word of God has so much to say concerning kindness to others. Read the following verses and make note of those to whom we are to show kindness.

Proverbs 14:31

____

Isaiah 1:17

____

Ephesians 4:32

____

1 Thessalonians 5:15

____

Helen Pearson says this concerning kindness: "The Lord can do great things through those who don't care who gets the credit."

In the next portion of this lesson, we will look at more truths concerning this fruit of kindness. Pray for a compassionate heart as we learn to live like the Kind One.

Day 2

Big Things in Small Packages

Our **Focus Verse** this week is a short fourteen words, but it speaks volumes. Write it below and commit to memorize it before our next lesson.

____

____

____

A kind word or small gesture of compassion does lift a person up, doesn't it? I want to begin today by sharing a story to illustrate the significance of seemingly small acts.

> A water bearer in India had two large pots; each hung on each end of a pole which he carried across his neck. One of the pots had a crack in it, and while the other pot was perfect and always delivered a full portion of water at the end of the long walk from the stream to the master's house, the cracked pot arrived only half full. For a full two years this went on daily, the bearer delivering only one and a half pots full of water to his master's house. Of course, the perfect pot was proud of its accomplishments. But the cracked pot was ashamed of its imperfection and sorry that it was not able to accomplish what it had been made to do.
>
> After two years, it spoke to the water bearer. "I am ashamed of myself and I want to apologize." "Why?" asked the bearer. "What are you ashamed of?"
>
> "I have been able to deliver only half my load because this crack in my side causes water to leak out all the way back to your master's house. Because of my flaws, you have to do all the work, and you don't get full value from your efforts," the pot said.
>
> The water bearer felt sorry for the old cracked pot, and in his compassion he said, "As we return to the master's house, I want you to notice the beautiful flowers along the path." Indeed, as they went up the hill, the old cracked pot took notice of the sun warming the beautiful flowers on the side of the path. But at the end of the trail, it still felt sad.

> The bearer said to the pot, "Did you notice that there were flowers only on your side of the path, but not on the other side? That's because I planted flower seeds on your side of the path, and every day while we walk back from the stream, you have watered them. For two years, I have been able to pick these beautiful flowers to decorate my master's table. Without you being just the way you are, he would not have this beauty to grace his house." Each of us is unique with our own flaws. We're all cracked pots. If we allow it, the Lord will use us in spite of our flaws to make flowers grow for someone to enjoy. You can be the cause of beauty in this world.
>
> —Author unknown, "The Cracked Pot"

This simple story illustrates the fact that small contributions, with God's blessing, can amount to great rewards. Never underestimate the impact your thoughtfulness will have on another.

Many Kindnesses Cost Nothing

Sometimes the kindest thing we can do for a cold, impersonal world is to spread loving smiles and a kind word to those we pass.

What is your reaction when someone smiles at you?

____

How does another's smile affect your interaction with them?

____

With a smile, we acknowledge to someone that they are important to us. Many people don't have a strong sense of self-worth or importance. Some have been so beaten down by abuse, neglect, or the pressures of life that they begin to doubt even the love of God. We as Christians may forget that life outside of Christ is a dark, hopeless place. We haven't lived in the desperate circumstances of many people today.

I love the African greeting I learned of recently. It goes like this: When a member of the tribe meets someone, he says, "I am here." The other person responds with, "I see you." Aren't those three little words wonderful? How much good can be done by acknowledging someone's presence on this earth! By sharing a warm smile, a kind word, or a listening ear, we just might break down barriers and provide a feeling of hope to the hopeless.

Kindness Is Never Wasted

King Solomon wrote, "Cast your bread upon the waters, for after many days you will find it again" (Ecclesiastes 11:1).

We should not expect to be compensated for showing kindness to another, but God is good; he always blesses us when we obey his word. Often, we receive the greater blessings from helping one another.

Can you think of a time recently when you were blessed as a result of a kind deed you performed?

____

____

____

The rewards for living a life in service to others are not always immediate or obvious. We may never know the good that comes from a simple act of grace. However, Jesus promised that if we would give, we would receive back in good measure, pressed down, shaken together and running over.

Kindness Sometimes Involves Risk

We mentioned at the beginning of this lesson that kindness is often the exception rather than the rule in our society. The reason for that may be because there are risks involved in helping others. It may involve more time than we have. It might mean we have to adjust our schedules. It could be that we need to spend a little money to provide for someone's need. Caring and sharing sometimes gets messy.

Remember the story Jesus told of the Good Samaritan in Luke 10:30–37? How did his decision to help the wounded man affect his plans for that day?

____

____

Kindness sometimes involves risk, but without risk there is no blessing. (I am not suggesting that you put yourself or your family in danger to assist a stranger. Always trust God's leading and use common sense.)

Read these inspiring words.

Be kind and merciful.

Let no one ever come to you

Without leaving better and happier.

Be a living expression of God's kindness.

Kindness in your face,

Kindness in your eyes,

Kindness in your smile,

Kindness in your warm greeting.

(Mother Teresa)

What a difference we could make in our world if we could live out those words!

God calls us to be light and salt on this earth. Both things enliven their surroundings. In tomorrow's lesson, we will get practical about our call to kindness. Prayerfully consider how you might better cause those flowers to bloom!

Day 3

Holy Habits

As we conclude this lesson on developing kindness, think about how you interact with others. Do you make a conscious effort to make others feel comfortable? Do you display common courtesy? Are you a good listener? Are you prepared to help those who may have need of material goods? How can you grow in this virtue of kindness?

In order to meet another's emotional or physical need, we must first become aware of it. This requires an attitude of service and a watchful eye. To answer the ancient question, "Am I my brother's keeper?" Yes! Take notice of when someone may be in need of encouragement. This may be in the form of a kind word or something more involved. You have to see the need before you can meet the need.

The Practice of Seeing

As we go about our busy lives, it is often difficult to be aware of anything outside of ourselves. Everyone has an agenda—a must-do list for the day. We flit from one place to another with only the next destination in mind. Kindness requires time. Time to see the faces and needs of another. Just like that African greeting, we must recognize the people around us, with words, smiles, and a willingness to enter into their circumstances.

It requires discipline to stop and notice others. Notice their faces, the tone of their voices, and their general states of being. See the frustration of the young mother with her small children in the store, trying to do three things at once. See the older gentleman sitting alone in worship service. See the new residents of the house next door on move-in day. Everyone has a story. Everyone has a need. Practice taking careful notice of the people around you today. Try to discover all you can about them in just a few seconds: what they're wearing, what they're doing, and the expressions on their faces. Take mental notes. You'll be surprised how much you have been missing.

Why do you think our society today has difficulty seeing?

____

The Practice of Listening

We made mention in lesson seven of the practice of listening and how it was an important ingredient in patience. Listening is key in showing kindness. Sometimes just listening to another as they share their troubles is the kindest thing we can do. Most of us do not really know how to listen. It involves more than just hearing sounds with our ears. When we truly listen with our hearts to the words of another, our entire body gets involved. Our eyes are locked on theirs. Our bodies are poised in a way as to lean in and give attention.

We will not formulate our response while the other person is still speaking. Listening involves putting aside all of our preconceived notions about the subject and withholding judgment until we have heard everything the other person has to say. It may also require repeating what we thought we heard for clarification. It will take discipline and intention to become a better listener. Begin today. Make a point to hear as much as you can of what the people you interact with have to say. Discipline yourself not to speak as much today. (This may be extremely difficult for some of us.) Don't forget to practice the body language of a true listener. See if you can pick up on the unspoken messages people send. Respond with a thoughtful word or reassuring gesture. Take action if need be in response to a perceived need.

Do you feel that you have a gift for listening? ______________________________

Can you identify any bad habits that may keep you from really hearing another person? _______
____

What new habits will you practice in order to grow in this area?

____

____

There's a familiar quip that says, "God gave us two eyes, two ears, and one mouth for a reason. Use them proportionately." As we come to a close on this lesson on kindness, pray that God will open your eyes and your heart to the needs of others. Ask him to give you the courage to risk inconvenience and to trust in his leading. Practice loving gestures as you seek to be Jesus to those you meet. As a result, God will send back blessings your way as well.

Continue to meditate on God's word as you pursue the godly nature he desires for you. Have a great week, sisters!

Dear Father in heaven,

I praise your Holy Name! You are a good and loving God. You have shown compassion on all you have made. You are faithful to all your promises. You delight in those who fear you. Please give me a compassionate love for my fellow man. May I determine to show kindness to all in response to your loving kindness to me. May I be your hands and feet and heart in this world.

Because of Christ's love,

Amen

For Additional Study

As I said earlier, there is so much in God's word concerning helping others. In order to give from a grateful heart, prayerfully read the following Scriptures describing God's kindness toward us. Then read Jesus' words concerning the judgment day.

Ephesians 2:4–9

Luke 6:35–36

Romans 2:4

Romans 11:22

What is your response after reading these verses?

____

____

____

Matthew 25:31–46

What would Jesus have to say concerning your response to the need of others?

____

LESSON 9

The Difference Maker:

Transforming Goodness

FOCUS VERSE

Ephesians 2:10

For we are God's workmanship, created in Christ Jesus to do good works which God prepared in advance for us to do.

Looking Back

I hope that since our last study you have had a fruitful week, bearing the fruit of kindness that is. I have noticed that when I make a point to speak to people pleasantly and smile at those with whom I come in contact, it causes my whole attitude to be more positive. It's difficult to stay in a blue mood when you are expending so much energy to encourage others.

This week we turn our attention to goodness. This high virtue goes hand in hand with the one we just completed. However, goodness takes it a step further. As we begin, pray for an attitude of readiness. The Christian life is not a solitary or stationary one. It calls for action and involvement in the lives of all of our neighbors. May God open our eyes to the good works he has prepared for us.

Day 1

Walk This Way

The idea of being a good person implies more than just treating someone with kindness. It is a disposition, an attitude, a way of living. In the analogy of the fruit tree, a heart purified by the spirit of God is a "good tree" which automatically bears good fruit or good deeds. It involves abstaining from evil practices as well as seeking to do good, to do what benefits mankind.

You may remember Jesus' encounter with the rich young ruler in Luke 18. What does Jesus tell him concerning goodness in verse 19?

____

____

So, how is it that we are to display a life of goodness?

Turn to 2 Peter 1:3–4.

What gives us the ability to do anything good or to be good?

____

What are we as Christians now able to participate in?

____

Now read verses 5–8.

Because of God's goodness toward us, what must we add to our faith?

____

Why is it necessary to add all these things to our faith?

____

Read Micah 6:6–8. What does the prophet say is "good."

____

____

____

Verse 8 is one of those nutshell Scriptures. God sums up so simply in this verse what it is that he would have us do to be pleasing to him. (One of those must-know scriptures!)

Act Justly

Why will a good person act justly?

____

____

____

To act justly is to do the right thing. It implies fairness and lawfulness. In the original Hebrew language, "dikaios" is translated into "fulfillment of duties toward gods and men." Justice is served when righteousness is followed.

How does Isaiah describe God in Isaiah 30:18?

____

Love Mercy

The second aspect of goodness is to love mercy. Mercy is showing more kindness than justice requires. Mercy goes the extra mile.

Jesus taught Peter a lesson about mercy through a parable in Matthew 18. Peter came to Jesus wanting to clarify just how many times he should forgive his brother. Feeling quite religious, Peter thought seven pardons would be more than enough. Jesus illustrated how ridiculous it is for us to presume innocence and to keep accounts with those who have wronged us.

What answer did Jesus give Peter in verse 22?

____

What did he mean by this answer?

____

A good person loves mercy and practices it freely, just as he would have Jesus be merciful to him.

Why is it often difficult to be merciful?

____

____

Walk Humbly

Lastly, in Micah 6:8, God desires for us to walk humbly with God. To recognize God's power and majesty in creating the universe and his compassion and mercy in coming down to earth to initiate a relationship with you and me necessitates our bowing humbly and considering our lowly estate. Isaiah records the Lord's words in his sixty-sixth chapter and verses one and two. Read these words and consider your proper place.

What are your thoughts after reading these words from our Father?

____

____

God esteems the humble and contrite in spirit. Jesus likened this type of attitude to that of a child in Matthew 18:4, and went so far as to say that it is only with that attitude that we will enter the kingdom of heaven.

Each of these three attributes mentioned in Micah 6 can come only with the help of the Holy Spirit. They are not natural to us as humans. They certainly are not what our society esteems as important or worthy of pursuit. Tomorrow's lesson will have more to say concerning the good works that have been prepared for each of us. This is where the rubber meets the road of our faith!

Day 2

Divine Assignments

In yesterday's study, we discovered three aspects of goodness from Micah 6. Today we will expand on those to see how we can carry out the plans that God has established for us.

Our **Focus Verse** for this week reminds us of our purpose on this earth. Write it below and commit it to memory before our next lesson.

____

____

____

Circle the four-word phrase in the verse above that tells why we were created.

James has a great deal to say about how our faith and our good works go hand in hand. Read James 2:14–18.

"What good is it, my brothers, if a man claims to have faith but ___________

_________ _______________?"

Faith that does not express itself in practical ways is of no value in God's eyes.

Consider the poem below.

I will do more than belong, I will participate.

I will do more than care, I will help.

I will do more than believe, I will practice.

I will do more than be fair, I will be kind.

I will do more than forgive, I will love.

I will do more than earn, I will enrich.

I will do more than teach, I will serve.

—Author Unknown, "I Will Do More"

We are called to be difference-makers in this life—to leave the world a better place because we have been here.

Many monuments have been erected throughout history to memorialize good men and women. For what types of acts are they usually honored?

____

____

____

A European Christian, Bridget Herman, had this to say about the saints of old:

> "When we read of the lives of the saints, we are struck with a certain leisure which went hand in hand with a remarkable effectiveness ... They did comparatively few things, and these not necessarily striking or important; and they troubled very little about their influence. Yet they always seemed to hit the mark ... their simplest actions had a distinction, and exquisiteness ... Their sainthood lay in their habit of referring the smallest actions to God. They lived in God; they acted from a pure motive of love towards God. They were as free from self-regard as from slavery to the good opinion of others ... They possessed God and they possessed themselves in God. Hence, the inalienable dignity of these meek, quiet figures that seem to produce such marvelous effects with such humble materials."

What are your thoughts concerning Ms. Herman's words?

____

____

____

____

Let's look at further instructions from God's word concerning goodness.

Read 2 Corinthians 9:8:

Why does God give so graciously to us?

____

____

Read 1 Timothy 6:17–19.

What happens when we are rich in good deeds, generous and willing to share?

____

____

____

Fill in the blanks of the scriptures below.

1 Peter 2:12:
"Live such good lives among the pagans . . . that they may see your good deeds and ________________ ________________ on the day he visits us."

Matthew 12:35:
"The good man brings good things out of the _____________ ___________ up in him."

Matthew 7:18–20:
"Every tree that does not bear good fruit _____________________________
____."

Galatians 6:9:

"Let us not become ________________ in ________________ ________________, for at the proper time we will reap a harvest if we do not __________ __________."

So how would you describe your fruit-bearing behavior lately?

Are you:

a. Still a little green b. Just beginning to flower

c. A bountiful harvest d. Mushy and beginning to rot

Peter tells us that we are to live such good lives that those who are unbelievers will see our good works and glorify God because of them. In tomorrow's lesson, we will identify some behaviors to help us see opportunities and accomplish those divine assignments God places before us. Bless you, my sisters!

Day 3

Holy Habits

I hope you have on your work gloves. Today we will get our hands dirty as we seek to cultivate those fruit trees. The fruit of our faith is the good work that God planned for us to do in his name before the beginning of time. Our lives should be rich in loving, giving, and encouraging.

As in the past, we will use the tools of discipline to train ourselves to be more effective in the kingdom of God. Pray over these suggestions, and ask God to reveal to you where you may need to do some weeding and feeding.

Recognize Opportunities

Often we neglect opportunities for service that God has placed before us because we don't have the proper mindset. We have gotten into a habit of assuming that someone else will take care of it and out of the habit of saying, "How will you have me serve you today, Lord?" Consider that if you are made aware of someone's need, it may be God's call to you to act. When in doubt, pray about the matter. God will make it clear to you if you are to help. James 4:17 says, "Anyone, then, who knows the good he ought to do and doesn't do it sins."

What opportunity has God placed before you in the last week to help another?

____

____

Train yourself to pray each day for clear vision to see the work God has for you that day. Whatever he asks you to do he will provide strength and resources to accomplish it. Step out in faith and ask.

Resist Excuses

Begin to recognize occasions where you make excuses for not doing the good you know to do. Remember Moses' excuses for not leading the Israelites out of Egypt? (Exodus 4) Remember Gideon's excuses for not leading the Israelites against the nation of Midian? (Judges 6) Remember Jonah's excuses for not preaching to the city of Nineveh? (Jonah 1) For every excuse they gave, God had an answer. Each time he told his servants that they did not go in their own strength, but in the strength of the Lord. He was not convinced by their earthbound reasoning. What would he say to you? With what divine assignment have you been struggling? Take every opportunity for good that comes to you, and present it to the Lord. Be honest about your hesitation or fear. God will calm your anxieties and provide you the strength you need.

What are the excuses you have made in the past for not doing something the Lord called you to do?

____

____

____

Satan will always be ready with one of his lies about your not being good enough or smart enough or any of a number of other reasons why you shouldn't follow the voice of God. Call him out! Realize his schemes and trust the Lord to lead you in the way he would have you go.

Get to Know People

Maybe you can't recall any opportunities lately. Are you making yourself available to people? Do you make it a point to be a part of the lives of your neighbors, coworkers, or those with whom you attend church? What avenues do you have that would cause your path to cross with others?

Try making the extra effort to find out how people are doing. Call to check on that coworker who has been out sick. Check on the elderly neighbor who lives alone. Sit by the visitor in church on Sunday. Find out if they have a need you can fill. Even a cup of cold water given in Jesus' name is a great gift.

For some of us, myself included, this means stepping out of our comfort zone. It may not come naturally to approach someone and inquire about his life. So many people are just waiting for a friend to show concern. They may feel embarrassed to share their need unless you give them the opportunity. Remember, we as Christian women are to be light and salt in this world. We are called to share the love of Christ daily. I like this little rhyme: "Only one life; 'twill soon be past; only what's done for Christ will last!"

As we close this week's lesson, make the commitment to pray for those around you—friends, neighbors, family, coworkers, the needy. Ask God to show you the good work he has prepared for you and to give you the courage to step out in faith, knowing that he will provide the resources for whatever he calls you to do.

Have a blessed week!

Dear Father in heaven,

You have blessed me with good things beyond my imagination. Even the unpleasant events of my life have brought about unexpected blessings. Help me to recall your faithfulness to me and to endeavor to live a life of service and blessing to those in my world. Make me sensitive to the needs of others and willing to enter their lives for your glory.

Through Christ I Pray,

Amen

For Additional Study

Read the 103rd Psalm of David. This is a wonderful reminder of all the good that the Lord has done for us. Count the number of times you read the word "compassion." When you finish, make a list of the good things in your life. Include the names of people who have had a profound impact on you. Give thanks.

LESSON 10

The Foxhole Friend:

Transforming Faithfulness

FOCUS VERSE

Lamentations 3:22, 23

Because of the Lord's great love we are not consumed,

for his compassions never fail. They are new every

morning; great is your faithfulness.

Looking Back

Welcome to our tenth week of study! It is exciting to think that we have spent the past nine weeks memorizing Scripture and learning to surrender ourselves to his transforming power. The task is daunting, for sure, but Christ partners with us in our endeavor. In Christ, we are more than conquerors! Let's press on this week in our study of transforming faithfulness.

The concept of faithfulness is such a broad one. It can apply to our relationships with God, with our family members, friends, even to the body of Christ. To which of these is the Apostle Paul referring when he lists faithfulness as being one of the fruit of the spirit in Galatians 5:22? I believe the answer is "all of the above." In this lesson, we will consider four different aspects of faithfulness:

The Faithfulness of God

Our Faithfulness to God

Our Faithfulness to Others

Our Faithfulness to the Body of Christ

Day 1

Rock Solid

It happens approximately every ninety minutes. It's been going on for hundreds of years. People stand in awe and watch it. What is it? The eruption of Yellowstone National Park's Old Faithful. This geyser, an amazing phenomenon of nature, spews boiling water as far as one hundred eighty feet into the air every hour and a half or so. On occasion, it happens as frequently as every forty-five minutes or as far apart as one hundred twenty-five minutes. But still, it stands true to its name, Old Faithful. Why was it named so? Because it can be relied upon to perform each and every day as expected. How many things in life can we say are truly faithful? Think about it. Cars break down, meetings are cancelled, people get sick, jobs fall through, and marriages fail. How does the saying go? "The only sure thing is that there are no sure things"? Well, that may be true of the world, but it is not true of our God. He calls us as his children to be true, to be sure, and to be faithful.

As we begin this study on faithfulness, let's think about what that word implies.

Write as many words as you can think of that describe faithfulness.

____

____

The Hebrew word for faithfulness is *emunah.* It is literally translated as "firmness." Webster's New World Dictionary defines faithfulness as: "steadfast adherence to a person or thing to which one is bound." I like that definition. The word steadfast carries with it the idea of continual activity, even through great difficulty. Faithfulness sometimes is difficult, isn't it? It is a decision to remain committed to someone or something, to follow through, to remain loyal, even when we don't have those feelings. It is a trait that God calls his people to grow in and one that he so beautifully has demonstrated throughout all of history. Let's begin our study today by rediscovering the faithfulness of our great God.

The Faithfulness of God

Of the myriad passages in the Bible referring to faithfulness, we see that overwhelmingly the majority speak in terms of the faithfulness of God to his people. After all, God never calls us to display any characteristic that is not first present in his own character.

From the earliest chapters recorded in Genesis, when God followed through with his promise regarding the Tree of Knowledge until the Crucifixion, when all the prophecies concerning the Messiah were fulfilled, God has remained true to his word and to his plans. Let's look at just a few of the promises he has made to us.

Deuteronomy 7:9: To what extent is God faithful?

____

Psalm 145:13b: To what is the Lord faithful?

____

1 Thessalonians 5:23–24: What does God promise to do for us?

____

1 John 1:9: What will God be faithful to do if we confess our sins?

____

Hebrews 13:8: What do we know for sure about Jesus?

____

Deuteronomy 32:4 records that: "He is the Rock, his works are perfect, and all his ways are just. A faithful God who does no wrong, upright and just is he."

There is a beautiful old hymn written by Thomas Chisholm called "Great is Thy Faithfulness." Read the chorus below and hear the confidence of a man who must have enjoyed a lifetime of God's faithfulness.

"Great is Thy faithfulness, O God my Father;
There is no shadow of turning with Thee;
Thou changest not, Thy compassions, they fail not;
As Thou hast been, Thou forever will be."

Let's look further at what the Psalmist had to say concerning the wonders of God's faithfulness.

Match each promise with the correct Scripture reference.

Psalm 57:10	a. *He abounds in love and faithfulness.*
Psalm 86:15	b. *His faithfulness endures forever.*
Psalm 91:4	c. *His love reaches to the heavens and his faithfulness to the skies.*
Psalm 117:2	d. *His faithfulness will be our shield.*

Write this week's **Focus Verse** on the lines below. Commit to memorize it before the next lesson.

____

____

____

____

Most recently, how has God proved himself faithful to you?

____

____

____

What does our Lord's great faithfulness mean to you?

____

____

____

How comforting to know that we serve a God who never changes. He doesn't fall in and out of love with us. We don't have to wonder what he expects of us from day to day. His ways are perfect. Hallelujah!

Our Faithfulness to God

There are several directives in Scripture to help us know what God expects of us concerning our faithfulness to him. The Hebrews writer speaks about this when he puts forth a call to persevere in our Christian faith. We are reminded that we have obligations and privileges that come with being washed in the blood of Christ.

Read Hebrews 10:19–39.

What four directives are given in verses 22–25? (Let us ...)

____

____

____

Verses 26–29 remind us that the faithful are to ruthlessly cast sin from their lives.

What is the final word concerning faithfulness in verses 38 and 39?

____

____

Our faithfulness to God is a direct function of our faith in God.

Matthew 25:14–30 records a story Jesus told of a man going on a journey. He calls his servants together and gives them each a portion of his money to take care of while he is away. We are told that he gave to each one according to his ability. No one was given more than was reasonable for him to handle. Each man had the capacity and skills to manage his share. Jesus tells that two of the three invested their shares and gained income for the master. The last man went and hid his portion in the ground in order to protect it. Read the master's response upon his return in verses 19–30.

Who did the master count as faithful? Why?

____

What adjectives did the master use to describe the third servant who gained nothing in verses 26 and 30?

What does this story tell us concerning God's view on faithfulness?

____

The servants in the story each received talents or portions of money. What might the talents represent today

____

____

We know that God wants us to be faithful in our giving of the material goods that he bestows on us, but he also expects us to use the abilities and skills that he designed within each of us to his glory and for his kingdom. Take a look at these words from the apostle Peter.

1 Peter 4:10

"Each one should use whatever gift he has received to serve others, ______________________________ __________________________ God's grace in its various forms."

God's plan for meeting the needs of people is for Christians to use the abilities and resources he gave them to be a blessing to others. Our failure to honor God with all he has given us—physically, emotionally, and spiritually is sin and we are like the wicked, lazy servant in the parable when we fail to use our talents, abilities, time, etc. as we should.

As we come to the end of today's study, pray that God will show you where you may be lacking in faithfulness to him. Ask for the courage to make it right.

Day 2

Firm to the End

Today we will turn our attention to how God expects us to remain faithful to others and to the body of Christ, his church. How we relate to others is, of course, also a function of our faithfulness to God.

Our Faithfulness to Others

Our Christian witness depends upon our reputation for honesty and integrity. Jesus said that we are to be like a city set on a hill. When people look at us they should see someone on whom they can depend? Are we where we say we will be when we say we will be there? Can we be trusted to follow through with the responsibilities we are given? Are we completely honest, even in the little things?

Go back to the words you wrote down to describe faithfulness at the beginning of this lesson. Do they describe you?

To what or to whom must we show ourselves faithful?

____

____

____

I recently read the story of Betsy Chalmers, a fifty-year-old woman from Richmond, Virginia. She met her husband at age nineteen and married at twenty. Two years into the marriage, her husband was convicted of a violent crime and sent to prison. Chalmers has spent thirty years being faithful to a husband she sees only four hours each weekend. They talk on the phone twice per week for twenty minutes. Chalmers explains, "I was mad, sad, disappointed and frightened, but I loved him and he needed me, so I stayed." She further adds, "I have come to the conclusion that it's not the life I have that defines me, it is the way I choose to live that life. I choose to live it by being faithful."

What a powerful example of devotion and loyalty. If we are to continue to grow in the likeness of the Father, we too must live such a life of integrity and faithfulness to others. You can be sure that the world is watching to see if we walk the talk.

Our world today is starving for people who cannot be bought, whose word is their bond, and who are honest in the small things as well as the large ones.

What are some excuses we sometimes give for unfaithfulness (of any type)?

____

____

____

Do you think unfaithfulness is a bigger problem today than in past generations? Explain.

____

____

____

Name someone that you can count on to be a faithful friend (other than the Lord).

____

What does it mean to you to have someone you can always count on?

____

____

____

Unfaithfulness always causes decay. This is true for relationships as well as habits and responsibilities. If we neglect to water our houseplants, they die. If we fail to put oil in our car, the engine will break down. If we do not keep our commitments to family and friends, the relationships will decay.

Solomon gives a humorous illustration of a serious truth about unfaithfulness in Proverbs 25:19. Write the verse on the lines below.

____

____

____

We know this to be true. Something or someone who is unfaithful, unreliable, and of questionable loyalty is of little or no use to us. The same is true with God.

Our Faithfulness to the Body of Christ

The last area we will look at is certainly not least in importance. The church is God's plan for carrying the message of the gospel to the entire world. Paul gives us great insight for how the church is to function in 1 Corinthians 12. Read verses 12–30.

In verse 12, we see that the body, though made up of many parts, is to function as a ____________________.

According to verse 18, how has God arranged all the parts?

____

According to verse 27, what is true of each one of us in the church?

____

We have a responsibility to our spiritual family to faithfully serve, encourage, and support them. This can only be done if we are meeting together regularly and becoming a part of each other's lives.

What are you blessed to be able to do in and for the church?

____

____

____

If nothing comes to your mind on the previous question, you need to go back to lesson two of this Bible study. As Paul said, we are all given gifts to use in the church. If we are not utilizing those gifts and abilities, we are crippling the Lord's work. It is just not an option.

On a more positive note, a church family that meets together regularly for periods of worship and fellowship and who strive together to accomplish a greater goal is a picture of heaven on earth. Christ died for this body of believers, and no group on earth has more reason to join hands and work together as brothers and sisters to serve others than we do.

Consider your relationship with your church family. If it is not one of cooperation and mutual blessing, I urge you to go to God and seek guidance and wisdom on what you can do to facilitate this type of relationship. It is a matter of your faithfulness to the Father.

In the final portion of this lesson, we will look at some ways to learn to be more faithful followers.

Day 3

Holy Habits

How to be a Foxhole Friend

We all want to be that individual who can be trusted to come through no matter what—whether with our spouse, our children, our church family, or with God. As with all godly virtues, it requires discipline. How can we train to be more trustworthy in all situations?

If it is true that our faithfulness to God is in direct proportion to our faith in God, we must strive to increase our faith. We know that faith comes from hearing the Word (Romans 10:17); consequently, to be a more faithful woman of God, we must be sure to spend time regularly in his word. A knowledge and sincere belief in God's word and in his power in our lives will, in turn, cause us to strive for more faithfulness to him.

In which area of life do you feel the need to be more faithful?

____

____

Are you spending regular time with the Lord in study and prayer?

____

Think back to the excuses you listed that we often give for failing to do what we should do. Can you identify with any of them? Which one(s)?

____

____

____

Take a look at some of the most common excuses we give and some spiritual disciplines that may help you in these areas.

"It's Just Not My Gift"

Maybe you tend not to do certain things because they are uncomfortable for you. Face it; there are some things that you just don't care for very much. After all, surely someone else can visit the nursing homes and hospitals. Those places are just not pleasant. Besides, it's just not your gift, right? Wrong!

Remember when God called Moses to do a task he didn't feel comfortable doing? He tried the excuse of, "It's not my gift. Maybe someone else should do it." God responded by proving to Moses that he would give him the ability, the wisdom, and the strength to do whatever he called him to do.

If an opportunity to serve comes to you and you feel God is leading you to do it, pray that God will provide a mentor or another person to go along with you the first few times. Believe that you can learn to do things you've never done before, and know that sometimes God intends for us to stretch our spiritual muscles in order to grow.

"Something Came Up"

A common excuse for not fulfilling a commitment is that something came up. We couldn't do what we said we would do because of something else we had to do. It's hard in today's world to fit it all in. As a matter of fact, it's impossible. There are times when we will not get everything done. However, if we've made a commitment to do something or to be somewhere at a certain time, we have an obligation to fulfill that responsibility before we do anything else.

Maybe better planning would have solved the problem. There are all kinds of day timers and personal calendars available these days that allow us to know at a glance what obligations we have before accepting others. Begin the day with an overview of the things you need to accomplish. Ask the Lord to bless the day and to give you wisdom to know what he would have you do in the hours you have.

Another tool to help you learn to be more faithful is to ask yourself these questions before saying "Yes."

1. Do I really understand this commitment?

2. How does this fit into my current goals and priorities?

3. Do I have the time and energy to do this?

4. What impact will this have in one year, in five years, in ten years?

5. Who will I help? Who will it hurt?

6. What do my friends and family think?

7. What would God have me do?

No Excuse

Many times our lack of faithfulness to God isn't something that happens intentionally. We just seem to slip into poor habits and before you know it, we've completely lost our way spiritually.

There are many things that can help get us back on track. First of all, we need to confess our unfaithfulness and repent. Decide to start anew and do the right thing. Remember, we didn't fall into bad habits overnight, and we also won't rectify the problem overnight. It will require an intentional and consistent effort to retrain ourselves. Begin by soliciting the help and support of a trusted friend to encourage you. Pray daily for the strength to make the right choices concerning how you spend your time and resources. Begin immediately in a daily Bible study routine. Set aside just a few minutes a day at first and meditate on a Scripture and pray over the day's activities. God will be faithful to bring you back into a right relationship if your heart is in the right place.

What steps will you take to discipline yourself to fulfill your responsibilities to the best of your ability?

____

____

I hope that this week's study has helped you to assess you own faithfulness in all your relationships. Commit to being a woman of integrity and practice becoming more trustworthy in the little things as well as the big ones. Have a great week!

Dear Father in heaven,

I praise you for your untiring faithfulness to me. I give thanks for your continual protection and provision. Place within me a sincere spirit of devotion and commitment when it comes to keeping my word and fulfilling my obligations. Teach me to remain steadfast and always trust in you.

In the name of my loving Jesus,

Amen

For Additional Study

Make a list of Bible characters that you can recall who exhibited a life of faithfulness to God even through adverse circumstances. Read their stories again, and make a list of any spiritual habits they employed that caused them to be more faithful.

LESSON 11

Easy Does It:

Transforming Gentleness

FOCUS VERSE

1 Peter 3:3, 4

Your beauty should not come from outward adornment,
such as braided hair and the wearing of gold jewelry
and fine clothes. Instead, it should be that of your inner self,
the unfading beauty of a gentle and quiet spirit,
which is of great worth in God's sight.

Looking Back

I hope you were blessed last week by our study on faithfulness. Have you found yourself paying closer attention to the commitments you make and being sure to show yourself faithful, even in the small things? Christian integrity speaks volumes to a world filled with deceitfulness and broken promises.

This week, we turn our attention toward gentleness, the next on the list of the fruit of the spirit from Galatians 5:22–23. As we continue to surrender our will to God's and allow him to transform our hearts into a better likeness of his, we must consider the beautiful trait of gentleness. There is no better word to describe the way our loving savior, Jesus Christ, interacted with the people he met. No doubt. That is one reason why so many were drawn to him. His tender and gentle spirit put people at ease immediately. They never felt shamed or burdened when they were with him, and they were never the same afterwards. Our **Focus Verse** for this week points out that a gentle and quiet spirit is what makes a woman beautiful in God's eyes.

Day 1

Fragile, Handle with Care

Write the words to the **Focus Verse** on the lines below. Commit to memorize them before the next lesson.

____

____

____

____

____

I like the eighteenth century theologian, J. A. Bengel's description of gentleness. He calls it a condition of the mind and heart: "Tranquility arising from within, creating no disturbance to others and bearing with tranquility the disturbances of others."

What a peaceful and satisfying way to live! The ability to live gently with others, not giving way to frustrations or creating disturbances, but peacefully allowing others to be themselves and mediating with tenderness.

What pictures does the word gentleness conjure up in your mind?

____

____

Peter described real beauty, the kind that God appreciates, as the product of a gentle and quiet spirit. How are gentleness and quietness related?

____

____

Does anyone in particular come to mind when you think of gentleness? What is it about this person that is gentle?

____

____

What is the opposite of gentleness?

____

Consider these thoughts:

"Gentleness corrects whatever is offensive in our manner" (Swiss theologian, Hugh Blair).

Do you agree? Explain?

____

____

____

"When you encounter difficulties and contradictions, do not try to break them, but bend them with gentleness and time" (Swiss clergyman, Saint Francis de Sales).

"Nothing is so strong as gentleness, nothing so gentle as strength" (Saint Francis de Sales).

How does gentleness require strength?

____

____

____

The English language has changed a great deal since the King James translation of the Bible was written. Gentleness was described as meekness hundreds of years ago. The word meekness carries with it the connotation of weakness or deficiency today. This is not at all what the original Greek word for gentleness, *prautes,* meant.

What did Jesus say concerning meekness in Matthew 5:5?

____

____

There is a story told of General George Washington. It seems that on one occasion while fox hunting with friends, Washington's horse jumped a stone wall and knocked off a stone. He immediately got off his horse and replaced the stone. A friend said to him, "You are too big a man to bother with that." Washington replied, "No, I am just the right size."

Aren't we all just the right size to emulate the meekness Christ?

What Gentleness Is Not

Passivity or inactivity

Avoiding all conflict

Cowardice

Refusal to stand up for anything

Never do we see evidence of Jesus displaying any of the above traits. When the Pharisees and teachers of the law confronted him on numerous occasions concerning his teaching or activities, Jesus always answered them with the authority of the Father and set their confused thinking straight. He lovingly confronted sinners and explained the truth. He knew his Father's plan and followed it with strong conviction. In our second session this week, we will observe the greatest example of gentleness that has ever been, that of our Lord Jesus Christ. His life on earth was defined by loving kindness, compassion, and gentleness.

In preparation, meditate on our **Focus Verse** for this week and get ready for a radical beauty makeover of the most divine kind!

Day 2

The Shepherd Mentality

As we consider how to become the beautiful women we were designed to be, we must examine the gentleness of our Savior. His pattern for tender living must be followed if we are to have the kind of effect on our world that would cause people to turn to Christ.

The Gentleness of Christ

The Psalmist David referred to the Lord as his shepherd, an analogy filled with meaning. He described in his 23rd Psalm the loving care of the shepherd as he gently guides the sheep along the path to green pasture and leads them beside still waters. The prophet Ezekiel also used the shepherd analogy when speaking of the Lord.

Ezekiel 34:12 says, "As a shepherd looks after his scattered flock when he is with them, so will I look after my sheep. I will rescue them from all the places where they were scattered on a day of clouds and darkness."

Jesus longs to be our gentle, loving shepherd. He even used this term referring to himself when he said, "I am the good Shepherd," in John 10:11.

Read what Jesus says in Matthew 11:28–30.

"Come to me, all you who are weary and burdened, and I will give you rest. Take my yoke upon you and learn from me, for I am ____________________ and ________________________ in ________________________, and you will find rest for your souls."

How does the gentleness of Christ give our souls rest?

____

____

____

Eugene Peterson's *The Message,* paraphrases verse 29 this way: "Keep company with me and you will learn to live freely and lightly."

Now that sounds like a life we could all get into! Jesus whispers gently to come to him and lay our burdens down—our relationship burdens, our job-related burdens, our financial burdens, but most importantly, our spiritual burdens. He calls us to leave our lives of sin and take on his yoke of freedom and peace.

Farmers know about yokes. They are heavy wooden frames fastened around the necks of two work animals to hold them together for pulling a plow or vehicle. Yokes were often used to hold people in slavery and submission. They were burdensome and oppressive. Jesus said his yoke was easy and his burden light. To wear his yoke, however, still requires submission to the Father's will.

Gentleness toward His Disciples

Jesus dealt gently with his disciples, who often misunderstood his teachings and confused the mission. Read one account from Luke 9:46–50.

What were the disciples arguing about?

____

Jesus could have responded harshly, having to explain to them again about the real kingdom. Instead, he brings a little child before them. What was his response to them?

____

Before Jesus' words had time to evaporate from the air, it seems the disciples were back at it. John points out that they had tried to stop a man from driving out demons in Christ's name because he wasn't one of the twelve. How did Jesus handle this?

____

____

____

Gentleness toward the Sick

The gentle spirit of our Lord also touched the lives of many who came to him for healing. Read these tender examples. Note the soft words and loving gestures of Jesus.

Matthew 8:2–4

____

Matthew 9:20–22

____

Mark 8:22–26

____

Gentleness toward Children

There were many occasions when Jesus used children in his teaching points. Each time, he dealt gently and respectfully with them. Take a look at these examples.

Matthew 18:3, Matthew 21:15–16, Mark 9:37.

What attitude did Jesus have towards children?

____

____

Gentleness toward Sinners

Maybe most shocking was Jesus' tenderness toward sinners. Read this touching account of a repentant woman in Luke 7:36–50.

How might this story have turned out differently if Jesus had taken the attitude of the Pharisee?

____

____

Our Call to a Gentle Spirit

The scriptures are abundant that give instruction on gentleness. Notice the various writers and circumstances.

Isaiah 32:17—Isaiah to a rebellious Israel:

"The effect of righteousness will be __________________ and confidence forever."

Philippians 4:5—Paul, to the church at Philippi:

"Let your ____________________ be evident to all."

Colossians 3:12—Paul to the church at Colosse:

"Therefore, as God's chosen people, holy and dearly loved, clothe yourselves with compassion, kindness, humility, ____________________ and patience."

1 Peter 3:15—Peter to persecuted Christians:

"... Always be prepared to give an answer to everyone who asks you to give the reason for the hope that you have. But do this with ______________________ and respect."

1 Timothy 6:11—Paul to Timothy:

"... flee from all this and pursue righteousness, godliness, faith, love, endurance and __________________________."

1 Peter 3:1—Peter to wives:

"Wives, in the same way be ______________________________ to your husbands so that if any of them do not believe the word, they may be won over without words by the behavior of their wives..."

(Submission of a wife toward her husband is an expression of gentleness.)

To display the gentle spirit of being Christ-like requires an understanding of God's grace on our behalf. We must come to the place where we realize that the ground is level at the foot of the cross. We all stand in need of every ounce of God's grace that he will offer us. It is by understanding all that we have put Jesus through because of our sins that we are able to humble ourselves to the place of submitting our perceived strength for the good of others. Gentleness begets gentleness.

Tomorrow's study will focus on the nuts and bolts of becoming a gentler person. God can tame even the strongest of personalities and use them to bring quiet gentleness to a rough, harsh world.

Day 3

Holy Habits

A gentle and quiet spirit comes from the heart of God. As we live in this world and fight the temptations of pride and selfishness, we must discipline ourselves in this virtue.

I'll share a personal story with you, sisters. I was always the kid in the class that felt the necessity to ask questions. As a matter of fact, I still do. I'm naturally curious, I guess. Sometimes it's not a question but an opinion I'd like to share. It seems I always have something that I have to say. My husband chides me for interrupting him when he's trying to tell me something just because I think I know what he's going to tell me. It's so hard to keep my thoughts to myself! But these habits have gotten me into trouble on more than one occasion as things would slip out of my mouth in ways I hadn't intended. Have you ever been there?

So several years ago after reading the text that is our **Focus Verse** for this lesson, I decided I should start praying for that gentle and quiet spirit. I would look around at several women that I admired for their gentle, soft-spoken ways and pray that God would make me like them. I was disappointed after what seemed like ample time for this transformation to take place, when I seemed to be the same old me. I finally gave up, resigned to be "the outspoken one" forever. I must say though, that when I began studying God's word more seriously and praying consistently that he would give me more self-control and mold me into his likeness in his good time, I can honestly say that I am seeing some difference. Here is what I have concluded about my own spiritual growth in this area.

One must:

See the need for change—let the Scriptures convict.

Study the word of God seriously—accept the commands, claim the promises, and believe God will do it.

Pray consistently and specifically—write down the specific goal and pray it often.

Become more aware of one's words—ask God to remind me to "take captive every thought."

Let go and let God—give over control to the transforming power of God.

Now, I won't kid you, I still struggle to be that quiet and gentle woman, but God has brought me a distance away from where I was, and he tells me we are not finished yet.

Let me clarify here that a gentle spirit does not consist only of controlling your tongue at the appropriate times. It comes down to an attitude. It is a way of interacting with people in an easy, delicate fashion—like a mother interacts with her infant baby. The following illustration is a good one.

A guide was taking a group of visitors through a factory. One of the points of interest was a giant steam hammer. The guide explained how the machine was capable of flattening an automobile. Then he put down a walnut and had the hammer break the shell without hurting the meat of the nut, demonstrating power under perfect control.

Jesus had the power to call ten thousand angels to rescue him from the cross, but he suppressed that power and chose to endure the suffering for our sake. We may have the knowledge, power, or authority to do and say things that would not be beneficial or in the best interest of others at times. That ability to interact in a controlled manner, to speak softly and act mildly, with humility and grace is gentleness. It is a trait that we can discipline ourselves to grow in.

When do you most struggle with having a gentle spirit?

____

____

____

What would a gentler spirit look like in your life?

____

____

____

When do tender words and actions mean the most to you?

____

____

As we close this lesson, I pray that you will examine your way of interacting with others. Do you need to do as I did and bridle your tongue more often? Do you need to count to five before responding in order to choose your words more carefully? Do you need to spend time meditating on God's gentleness with you? Maybe you need to spend time observing gentle women. As someone has said, "Hang around with people who have fruit on their tree." I dare say all of these would be good habits to implement.

Which of the exercises listed in this lesson do you need to employ in order to strive for that unfading beauty?

____

____

____

Next week, we finish our study on transformation with a look at developing self-control. It is such an important virtue for the Christian woman! Meet me in the book of Galatians, and together we will discover how to live in the Spirit. Have a blessed week!

My loving Father in heaven,

Thank you for your tender touch in my life. You have been faithful to all your promises and loving toward all you have made. The gentle beauty of the rose's petals and the butterfly's wings remind me of your care for me. As the shepherd watches over his sheep, so you watch over my life. May I wait patiently and humbly for you as you mold me into the beautiful, gentle woman you desire me to be.

Through Jesus my Savior, I pray,

Amen

For Additional Study

The short book of James has much to say concerning our interaction with others. Read through the five chapters in one sitting, if possible. As you read, make a running list of actions that, when implemented, will improve your gentleness quotient. (You might find some great memory work here!)

LESSON 12

Get a Grip:

Transforming Self-Control

FOCUS VERSE

Galatians 5:16

Live by the Spirit and you will not gratify

the desires of the sinful nature.

Looking Back

I hope that you can say that you are feeling more beautiful than ever! The unfading kind of beauty, that is. Our **Focus Verse** from last week reminded us that our beauty should not come from outward adornment, but rather from a gentle and quiet spirit. This is what a beautiful woman looks like in God's eyes. May God bless you as you continue to develop a spirit of gentleness.

This week, we will begin considering the final fruit of the spirit given in Galatians 5. The fruit of self-control is a very important one. The possession (or lack) of it, affects a number of other characteristics in our lives. I'd better warn you, this lesson may call for some steel-toed boots! (I can already feel my toes being stepped on.)

Day 1

The Lifestyle of Fools

As usual, we must begin by defining the concept of self-control. Some would call it willpower—a decision of the will to do what is right, or to refrain from doing what is harmful to ourselves or to others.

Look at the following list and circle those qualities which require a certain degree of self-control.

Love

Joy

Peace

Patience

Kindness

Goodness

Faithfulness

Gentleness

Without self-control, it is unlikely that we will be able to display any of the other fruits of the spirit. Self-control requires us to reign in our desires and urges, giving thought before acting. It is what enables us to follow the laws of the land, maintain relationships, and protect ourselves from being carried away by emotion.

Within our makeup are God-given desires and urges which are given for our good. Many times, however, we allow those urges free reign, disregarding the parameters of Scripture, and neglecting the needs or desires of those around us.

We can all relate to the concept of something being out of control. Remember those white-knuckled scenes from television and movies where an automobile, train, or airplane runs out of control? Terror strikes our hearts on such occasions as we imagine the disastrous outcome.

It takes only minutes for a fire to spread to the point of being out of control. Floodwaters are capable of sweeping away the unsuspecting as they rush out of control.

God created an order to our world, and we simply aren't made to live in a state of disorder. So we must continually strive to keep our desires in check, to be in complete control of our words and actions, and to possess the presence of mind to make intentional choices.

Emily Battaglia, staff writer for Lifescript.com, in her article entitled, "I Just Can't Help Myself: Learning Self- Control," writes, "If you would live your life with ease; do what you ought, not what you please." It sounds almost biblical, doesn't it? It is a concept we try to teach our children, but often, we adults find it hard to follow.

Many times, we make poor choices in life because we have not decided in advance to make wise choices. It is those impulse buys, those careless words, and those unplanned sexual encounters that cause us so much trouble down the road. Write the words of our **Focus Verse** for this week on the lines below and commit to memorize them before the next lesson.

____

____

____

Paul says that the way to deny the desires of our sinful nature is to live by the Spirit. We all know, as did Paul, this is not an easy task. If we read further in Galatians 5, verse 17, it tells why it is not easy. Fill in the blanks.

Galatians 5:17

"For the sinful nature desires what is ________________________ to the Spirit, and the Spirit what is ________________________ to the sinful nature. They are in ____________________ with each other, so that you do not do __________________ __________________ ________________________."

We desire to follow the Spirit, but our sinful nature is strong within us. Paul experienced this struggle himself, which he recorded for us in his letter to the Romans. Paul explains that the purpose of the Jewish law was to identify sin. Look carefully at Romans 7:4–25. Read this passage slowly in order to digest Paul's lengthy explanation.

What words does Paul use to describe himself in verse 14?

___

Reread verse 18. Have you ever said this?

How does Paul describe what is going on between the members of his body and his mind in verse 23?

___

Someone referred to self-control as "the discipline of the soul."

Do you think this is an accurate assessment? Why or why not?

___

___

___

Our soul is the seat of all of our emotions and desires. It is who we are. As children of God, created in his image, we have a deep longing for the things of God. However, our human nature longs to have our fleshly desires fulfilled. Our soul struggles between good and evil. This is why God reminds us over and over in his word to live in the Spirit, not to conform to the world, to fix our eyes on the holy, and to discipline our souls.

We will leave our text in Romans for now and come back to it later.

Let's look at some of the wise teachings concerning self-control from the book of Proverbs. In your own words, make a note of the warning in each verse.

11:22

___

12:16

13:3

16:23

16:32

17:28

18:2

19:19

25:28

29:11

In Proverbs 1:3, we see that these sayings were all written in order to help us "acquire a disciplined and prudent life." They certainly paint an unflattering picture of the individual lacking self-control, don't they? More than once, this type of person is described as a "fool."

Solomon was credited with writing many of the proverbs we read above. However, he didn't always use the wisdom God gave him to control his fleshly desires.

What was Solomon's confession in the first part of Ecclesiastes 2:10?

____

____

What did Solomon conclude from this (2:11)?

____

His pursuit of every pleasure and his many wives brought him little joy and much heartache.

Another unfortunate incident is recorded in Numbers 20:1–13. Briefly explain Moses' sin at Meribah.

____

____

What was the result of Moses' behavior?

____

____

On yet another occasion, a young man made a foolish choice in the heat of the moment that affected the rest of his life. Read Esau's story in Genesis 25:27–34.

What did Esau trade to his brother, Jacob, for a bowl of soup?

____

Our moments of indiscretion don't always cost us as dearly, but some have indeed lost families, homes, jobs, and more due to their lack of self-control.

In the next session, we will investigate a few specific areas where we often find self-control difficult. We will see what God's word has to say concerning our fleshly desires. Here's where it gets personal!

Day 2

A Good Thing Gone Bad

Our **Focus Verse** for this lesson gives us a wonderful prescription for keeping our desires in check. When we learn how to live under the Spirit's power, we will be able to say no to the sinful cravings of man.

The Apostle John gives further instruction on living by the Spirit in 1 John 2:15–17. Listen to how Eugene Peterson paraphrases it in *The Message.*

> "Don't love the world's ways. Don't love the world's goods. Love of the world squeezes out love for the Father. Practically everything that goes on in the world—wanting your own way, wanting everything for yourself, wanting to appear important—has nothing to do with the Father. It just isolates you from Him. The world and all its wanting, wanting, wanting is on the way out—but whoever does what God wants is set for eternity."
>
> 1 John 2: 15–17, Msg

Focusing more on our own desires rather than on God's will for our lives leads to sin and destruction. 1 John 2:16 says it this way, "For all that *is* in the world, the lust of the flesh, and the lust of the eyes, and the pride of life, is not of the Father, but is of the world (KJV).

The Lust of the Flesh

God placed certain urges and desires within us for our good and for our protection. Sometimes we overindulge those desires, as when we harm our bodies by eating more than we should or eating the wrong things. This is a good desire gone out of control. We cannot glorify God when we allow our physical cravings to overpower us.

So also the sexual desire was intended to provide the motivation needed for our procreation. It was also a gift of God for the enjoyment of a man and woman within a marriage relationship.

Mankind has twisted these natural urges and used them for perverted and immoral purposes. When satisfied in an unhealthy or self-indulgent manner, our natural urges lead to sin.

Mark Twain said, "There is a charm about the forbidden that makes it unspeakably desirable."

Why are we drawn to the forbidden?

____

____

Paul in his letter to the Corinthians said that he had to "beat his body and make it his slave" (1 Corinthians 9:27).

What did Paul mean?

____

____

The Tongue

One area that often requires a beating is our tongue. James in his letter says if anyone is never at fault in what he says, he is a perfect man (3:2).

How does he describe the tongue in James 3:6?

____

What further observation does he make in verse 8?

____

This sobering assessment should make us ever vigilant in keeping a constant check on our words. So much good can be done with our words, but so much harm as well. It seems that, as women, we battle with this temptation more than men. The very fact that we find speaking so much more necessary than men do offers more opportunity for gossip, slander, and unsolicited opinions. Our speech should always reflect humility and gentleness and bring glory to God.

The Lust of the Eyes

It goes against the grain of our society to deny ourselves anything we see and desire. We are told in the marketplace that we can have it all. Whether you can afford it all or really need it all is simply not the issue. There are more opportunities in America to shop and spend than ever before. We don't even have to leave the comfort of our homes to do it. The Internet even allows us to spend without the nuisance of going through the physical exchange of currency.

According to Federal Reserve reports, total consumer credit stood at a record $2.54 trillion in February 2007. We buy even when we can't pay. Spending, for many people, has gotten out of control.

Do you sometimes find yourself shopping when you can't afford to or when you don't need anything?

Some have said they even find themselves getting an adrenaline rush from buying.

The Prince of this world delights in seeing us move farther away from recognizing God as the center of our lives and by indulging our own selfish desire for things.

Psychologist Walter Mischel in his classic experiment from the 1970s used a group of four-year-old children to test their ability to delay gratification. He placed each one in a room by themselves with a bell and a marshmallow. The children were told that if they rang the bell, the instructor would come into the room and the child could have the marshmallow. If, however, they would wait for the instructor to return on his own, they would be given two marshmallows. The results varied. Some children rang the bell in less than a minute. The most disciplined waited as long as fifteen minutes.

It was noted that those who delayed gratification did not sit and stare at the marshmallow, but rather they occupied themselves by doing something else to pass the time. (A good piece of advice for us!)

The experiment followed the progress of these children for several years. Some interesting results were found. Those who waited longer for the marshmallows scored higher on their college entrance exams, got into better colleges, and led more successful adult lives. Young people who were able to delay gratification were able to avoid drugs and alcohol. Those who weren't often dropped out of school and made a series of foolish decisions in their lives.

The Pride of Life

You'll remember that God hates pride in us. The Bible offers many warnings to the proud.

Why is pride so detestable to the Lord?

____

Satan's very downfall originated with pride. He let his own desire to be like God rule his mind. Though we may think that we would never go so far as to set ourselves up in God's place, we do this very thing when we ignore God's word and seek our own glory rather than his. It happens so subtly that we don't even recognize it sometimes.

The New International Version of the Bible translates "the pride of life" in 1 John 2:16 to mean "the boasting of what man has or does." To refer to James' writing again, he warns us not even to boast about what we plan to do tomorrow (James 4:13–16).

Christ—Our Perfect Example

Jesus showed us what a life under the control of the Holy Spirit should look like. Before beginning his ministry, he was led into the desert for a period of fasting and prayer for forty days, denying his physical needs in order to fully embrace the mission that lay before him. Later, he demonstrated great restraint when facing his imprisonment and death.

Read what the prophet Isaiah foretold in Isaiah 53:7.

"He was oppressed and afflicted, yet he ____
____________; He was led like a lamb to the slaughter, and as a sheep before her shearers is silent, so he ____."

We know that Jesus was completely human while living on this earth and he felt the same fear, pain, and fleshly desires that we experience, though he always remained in control of his emotions and actions.

I like the words of the Italian author and playwright, Pietro Aretino: "I am indeed a king, because I know how to rule myself."

What a job we have, learning to rule over our own fleshly desires!

What does Jesus say concerning the lack of self-control on the part of the Pharisees in his scathing remarks in Matthew 23:25?

____

____

____

The Good News

Mischel's marshmallow experiment concluded that differences in the ability to exercise control emerge early in life. It is not conclusive as to how much of the ability is hereditary and how much is environmental. The good news is that, with persistent effort, the ability to exercise self-control can be improved.

Again, referring to Romans 8:28–39, we see a most encouraging word from Paul!

Enjoy, believe, and claim the promises below.

Verse 28: "... in all things God works ________ _________ _________ of those who love him, who have been called according to his purpose."

Verse 31: "What, then, shall we say in response to this? ________ _________ _____ _________ __________, who can be against us?"

Verse 37: "... in all things we are _____________ _____________ ________________ through him who loved us."

There is no one who wants to see us succeed in conquering our demons more than Jesus Christ! He is ready and waiting to come to our aid when we call on him.

As we close today's lesson, take comfort in these words. Hebrews 4:15: "We do not have a High Priest who is unable to sympathize with our weaknesses, but we have One who has been tempted in every way, just as we are—yet was without sin."

Share your struggles with him and pray for strength to get through the hard times.

Day 3

Holy Habits

The topic for this week's study has been a heavy one. It strikes very close to home to think about denying ourselves. We know that nothing should stand between us and the God we serve, even our own desires. How can we train ourselves to just say no to self and seek God's will for our lives? This is at the very heart of discipline. We will know that we are becoming his when we think first of Jesus and not of ourselves. Now comes the practical part.

What are the areas of your life in which you lack self-control?

____

____

____

* Note: We need to mention here that if you struggle with an addiction that has taken a real stronghold in your life, you may need to seek professional help from a qualified counselor or medical personnel.

The first step in conquering a stronghold in our lives is to name it and claim it. Once we can face up to our spiritual weaknesses, we can begin to make a plan for retraining our thought processes. When we retrain our thoughts, we change our attitudes and then our actions.

Affirmations

One exercise that may help in your attempt to overcome a strong urge is to write your good intention in the form of an affirmation to read several times during the day. An affirmation is simply a positive statement that you declare to be true. For example, if you struggle with driving the speed limit when you're late for work, you might write something like this: "Driving the speed limit is the law of the land. I know that it provides the safest means for people to arrive at their destinations. I will drive the speed limit to honor God and to ensure my own safety and that of others."

It may be that you need to memorize and recite this affirmation several times a day or even spend a few moments meditating over it before starting the car. This helps to change how we think about driving and gives us the proper motivation for changing a bad habit.

Accountability Partners

Facilitators of twelve-step programs know the importance of accountability. One of the biggest reasons people fail in their resolutions is that they try to go it alone without sharing their commitment with others or asking someone to regularly hold them accountable.

Try writing down your resolution and sharing it with a trusted friend. (Friends often work better than family members because those who love us the most may not challenge us strongly enough.) Ask the friend to check in with you at least once a day to question you about your progress. Agree upon a penalty and reward for those good and bad days. Pray together regularly about your challenge.

Ecclesiastes 4:9–12 shares a great truth about partners.

> "Two are better than one, because they have a good return for their work: If one falls down, (her) friend will help (her) up! But pity the (woman) who falls and has no one to help (her) up! Also, if two lie down together, they will keep warm. But how can one keep warm alone? Though one may be overpowered, two can defend themselves. A cord of three strands is not quickly broken."

As we close this lesson and the twelfth week of our study, it is my prayer that you will begin making a plan for conquering those strongholds in your life. Trust God to empower you to break through to spiritual freedom in Christ. It was never his intent for you to be enslaved to your own desires. He wants you to enjoy all the riches of the abundant life, a life of love, joy, peace, patience, kindness, goodness, faithfulness, gentleness, and self-control.

I want to leave you with one more word of encouragement from the apostle Paul. This time it's from Galatians 5:8–9.

> "The one who sows to please his sinful nature, from that nature will reap destruction; the one who sows to please the Spirit, from the Spirit will reap eternal life. Let us not become weary in doing good, for at the proper time we will reap a harvest if we do not give up."

Persevere! Don't give up! Become the beautiful woman of God's dreams!

Dear Father,

I know that you desire to be the center of my life. You created me to glorify you in all things. You are worthy of all praise and honor. I confess that many times it is my own selfish desires that come before you. Please forgive me when I fail to put you first. I need your strength to help me flee temptation and to live for you alone. Guard my lips and sweeten my words. May I long for your Word rather than for material goods. Give me a grateful heart to see my blessings and lead me in the way everlasting.

In Christ, my Savior's name,

Amen

For Additional Study

The short Old Testament book of Ruth is a great study in one woman's unselfish decision to put aside her own needs and desires for the good of another. Read these four chapters and notice God's blessing for her faithfulness. Her quiet, controlled way will inspire you.

LESSON 13

Becoming Myself, Becoming His:

Personal Reflection

As we come to the final week of our studies, we will take an overall look at the various topics concerning spiritual transformation that we have explored.

It is my prayer that you can clearly identify specific areas where you have experienced real growth. I hope that you can say with confidence, "My life is no longer my own, it is his." God created you for a divine purpose, and he wants to work out his will through you, my sweet sister. Continue to apply discipline to your life as you grow in holiness. Rejoice in the faithfulness of your Father in heaven and remember that he loves you beyond measure!

God's richest blessings to you!

For each lesson, complete the **Focus Verse** and answer the questions as honestly as you can.

Lesson 1

Who Am I?

What Was God Thinking When He Created Me?

Psalm 139:23–24

"Search me, O God and ____;

test me and ____.

See if there is ____,

and lead me ____."

Your heavenly Father makes a point to know you completely. What is one thing you have discovered about yourself through this study?

____

____

Lesson 2

Sweet Dreams:

Does God Really Have a Plan for My Life?

Jeremiah 29:11

"For I know ____,"

declares the Lord, "plans to ____

and not to ____________________________________, plans to give you

__________________ and a ____________________________."

God put within each of us certain desires and skills to be used for his glory and for the kingdom. What holy task do you feel you must do?

____

____

____

____

Lesson 3

Becoming:

How Can I Be Transformed into His Likeness?

Romans 12:2

"Do not _________________________________ to the pattern of this world, but

be ____.

Then you will be able to ____

____—His good,

pleasing, and perfect will."

It has been said, "Discipline is an avenue to holiness, and holiness is the key to joy and peace." In what area of your life do you need to practice more discipline?

____

____

____

Lesson 4

What the World Needs Now:

Transforming Love

Galatians 5:22–23

"But the fruit of the spirit is ___________________________________

____

____."

It has been said, "To spend little time with Jesus is to accomplish little in Jesus."

How would spending more time with Jesus allow you to be more of the woman God intended you to be?

____

____

____

____

Lesson 5

The God Who Smiles:

Transforming Joy

Psalm 100

"Shout for joy to the Lord, all the earth. ________________________________

____

____.

Know that the Lord is God. ____

____

and ______________________________________. We are the sheep of His pasture. Enter His gates ____

and His courts _______________________________________; give thanks to Him and praise His name. For _____________________________________

and ____;

His faithfulness ____

____."

By focusing on contentment, we can find greater joy in our lives. In what area do you need to cultivate contentment?

____

____

____

Lesson 6

Sleeping Like a Baby:

Transforming Peace

Proverbs 3:5–6

"Trust in the Lord with all your heart, and ______________________________

____;

in all your ways ____,

and ____."

Jesus tells us in Matthew 6:27 that we should not worry but rather seek the kingdom of heaven. What spiritual habits do you have that help you seek the kingdom at this point in your life? Be specific.

____

____

____

Lesson 7

Ladies in Waiting:

Transforming Patience

Ephesians 4:2

"Be completely ________________________ and _______________________;

be __________________________, bearing with _________________________

__________________________."

The concept of patience is multifaceted, involving patience with ourselves, those around us, and with God. In which of these areas do you need to cultivate a greater degree of patience? Explain.

____

____

____

____

Lesson 8

Living a You-First Life in a Me-First World:

Transforming Kindness

Proverbs 12:25

"An anxious heart ____,
but a kind word ____."

Jesus tells us in the twenty-fifth chapter of Matthew what the judgment scene will look like. The King will divide the sheep from the goats according to their response to the needy and unfortunate of the world. Who do you know that is in need of a cup of cold water today?

____

Lesson 9

The Difference Maker:

Transforming Goodness

Ephesians 2:10

"For we are God's workmanship, created in Christ Jesus ____________________

____

____."

Paul said in 2 Corinthians 9:8 that God gives graciously to us so that we will do good works on behalf of others. Is the way you manage your money preventing God from doing more in your life? Explain.

____

____

____

Lesson 10

The Foxhole Friend:

Transforming Faithfulness

Lamentations 3:22–23

"____

we are not consumed, for His ______________________________________

____________________________________. They are new every morning;

great is Thy faithfulness."

In the parable of the talents in Matthew 25, Jesus teaches that God expects us to use the gifts he gives us for his glory. How are you glorifying him through your talents?

____

____

____

Lesson 11

Easy Does It:

Transforming Gentleness

1 Peter 3:3–4

"Your beauty should not come from outward adornment, such as braided hair and the wearing of gold jewelry and fine clothes. Instead:

____

____

____."

God's word frequently encourages us to deal gently with people. Colossians 3:12 describes it as "being clothed" with gentleness. Who in your life most needs your gentle touch now?

____

Lesson 12

Get a Grip:

Transforming Self-Control

Galatians 5:16

"Live by the Spirit and you will not __________________________________."

Hebrews 4:15 says that Jesus, our High Priest, was tempted in every way, just as we are. Picture him struggling with one of your weaknesses. What would Jesus do?

____

____

____

____

A FINAL WORD

My sisters, wake up and expect God to work through you today! Spend the most important few minutes of your day with him in prayer and meditation on his word. Ask him to mold you and shape you until you are a better likeness of him. Continue to apply discipline to your life in order to pursue precious holiness. Rejoice in the goodness and faithfulness of your Father in heaven. Become his loving and devoted daughter.

God's richest blessings to you!

FURTHER READING

Addicott, Jaramillo, and Moore. *The Macalester Undergraduate Behavioral Neuroscience Project.* St. Paul: Macalester College, 2003.

Alexander, David, and Pat. *Eerdman's Handbook to the Bible.* Grand Rapids: William B. Eerdman's Publishing, 1973.

Alton, Howard. *Songs of Faith and Praise.* West Monroe: Howard Publishing, 1994.

Battaglia, Emily. "Your Health, Your Life, Your Way." Lifescript.com.

Blair, Hugh. Quote, Brainyquotes.com.

Bales, Norman. *He Died to Make Men Holy.* Joplin: College Press Publishing, 1991, 328.

Brooks, David. "Self-Control is the Key to Success." New York Times Service, May 9, 2006.

Chalmers, Betsy. "The Story of Betsy Chalmers." This I Believe Essays. NPR.org.

Cloninger, Claire. *Joy for the Journey, A Woman's Book of Joyful Promises.* Dallas: Word Publishing, 1997.

Copeland, Germaine. *Prayers that Avail Much for Mothers.* Tulsa: Harrison House, 1990.

Duckworth, Lisabeth. *Bloom Before You're Planted: Gardening Tools for a Woman's Soul.* Colorado Springs: Cook Communications Ministries, 2007.

Enrichmentjournal.com. George Washington story.

George, Elizabeth. *Putting on a Gentle and Quiet Spirit.* Eugene: Harvest House, 2000.

Gray, Stephens, and Van Diest. *Lists to Live By.* Sisters: Multnomah, 1999, pp. 84, 225.

Hawley, Monroe. *The Focus of Our Faith.* Nashville: Twentieth Century Christian

Foundation, 1985, 79.

Heynan, Ralph. *The Art of Christian Living: Christian Faith and Mental Health.*

Grand Rapids: Baker Book House, 1963, 37.

Hill, Debbie. *Survey of Gifts.* Gateway Church of Christ, 2008.

Jeffress, Robert. *The Road Most Traveled: Releasing the Power of Contentment in Your Life.* Nashville: Broadman and Holman Publishing, 1996.

Kelly, John. *A Testament of Devotion.* New York: Harper Brothers, 1941, 54.

Le Fevre, Perry. *The Prayers of Kierkegaard.* Chicago: University of Chicago Press, 1956, 147.

Lucado, Max. *Just Like Jesus.* Nashville: Word, 1998, 136.

Lucado, Max. *Let the Journey Begin: God's Roadmap for New Beginnings.*

Nashville: Word, 1998, 53.

MacDonald, Gordon. *Ordering Your Private World.* Nashville: Moody Press, 1984, pp. 30–31, 144.

McCleary, Mac. Patience. Quotegarden.com.

Merriam-Webster's Online Dictionary. 2005.

New Concise Webster's Dictionary. New York: Modern Publishing, 1989, 308.

Ortberg, John. *If You Want to Walk on Water, You've Got to Get Out of the Boat.* Grand Rapids: Zondervan, 2001, 58, 60.

Ortberg, John. *The Life You've Always Wanted.* Grand Rapids: Zondervan, 2002, pp. 83, 84.

Partow, Donna. *A Ten-Week Journey to Becoming a Vessel God Can Use.* Grand Rapids: Bethany House, 1996, pp. 191, 197.

Perlman, Myer. *How to Speak Effectively.* Springfield: Gospel Publishing House, 1949, 51.

Peterson, Eugene. *The Message.* 2 Corinthians 3:18, Matthew 11:29, Colorado Springs: Navpress, 2000.

Prentiss, Elizabeth. *Stepping Heavenward: One Woman's Journey to Godliness.* Uhrichsville, Barbour Publishing, 1998.

Rosen, Darryl. *Surviving the Middle Miles: 26.2 Ways to Cross the Finish Line.* Bloomington: Authorhouse, 2007.

Saint Francis de Sales. Quote. Brainyquotes.com.

Sanders, J. Oswald. *Every Life is a Plan of God.* Nashville: Discovery House, 1992, 11.

Spurgeon, Charles. *Treasury of David Commentary.* Bibleclassics.com, Psalm 139.

Strong, James. *Strong's Talking Hebrew Dictionary.* Wordsearchbible.com, Austin, 2002, 3068.

Swindoll, Charles. *Stones of Remembrance, Bible Study Guide.* Anaheim:

Insight of Living, 1988, 5.

Thompson Chain Reference Bible Book Outlines. Leadership Ministries Worldwide, 2002, 4250.

Thefreedictionary.com. Meekness.

The Holy Bible: New International Version. Grand Rapids: Zondervan, 1988.

Wallis, Claudia. "Stress: Can We Cope?" Time Magazine. 6 June, 1983, pp. 48–54.

Warren, Rick. *The Purpose Driven Life.* Grand Rapids: Zondervan, 2002, 18.

Webster's Thesaurus. Ashland: Landoll, Inc. 1997, 115.

Wikipedia, The Free Encyclopedia. Old Faithful Geyser, 228.

Wilkinson, Bruce. *Set Apart: Discovering Personal Victory through Holiness.*

Sisters: Multnomah Publishers, 1998, pp. 167, 181.

Wirt, Sherwood. *Jesus, Man of Joy.* Eugene: Harvest House, 1999, pp. 45–46.

Focus Verses

FOCUS VERSE

Psalm 139:23-24

Search me, O God, and know my heart; test me and know my anxious thoughts. See if there is any offensive way in me, and lead me in the way everlasting.

FOCUS VERSE

Jeremiah 29:11

"For I know the plans I have for you," declares the Lord, "plans to prosper you and not to harm you, plans to give you hope and a future."

FOCUS VERSE

Romans 12:2

Do not conform any longer to the pattern of this world, but be transformed by the renewing of your mind. Then you will be able to test and approve what God's will is - his good, pleasing and perfect will.

FOCUS VERSE

Galatians 5:22, 23

But the fruit of the Spirit is love, joy, peace, patience, kindness, goodness, faithfulness, gentleness and self-control.

FOCUS VERSE

Psalm 100

Shout for joy to the Lord, all the earth. Worship the Lord with gladness; come before him with joyful songs. Know that the Lord is God. It is he who made us, and we are his; we are his people and the sheep of his pasture.

Enter his gates with Thanksgiving and his courts with praise; give thanks to him and praise his name. For the Lord is good and his love endures forever; his faithfulness continues through all generations.

FOCUS VERSE

Proverbs 3:5, 6

Trust in the Lord with all your heart, and lean not on your own understanding; in all your ways acknowledge him, and he will make your paths straight.

FOCUS VERSE

Ephesians 4:2

Be completely humble and gentle; be patient, bearing with one another in love.

FOCUS VERSE

Proverbs 12:25

An anxious heart weighs a man down, but a kind word cheers him up.

FOCUS VERSE

Ephesians 2:10

For we are God's workmanship, created in Christ Jesus to do good works which God prepared in advance for us to do.

FOCUS VERSE

Lamentations 3:22, 23

Because of the Lord's great love we are not consumed, for his compassions never fail. They are new every morning; great is your faithfulness.

FOCUS VERSE

1 Peter 3:3, 4

Your beauty should not come from outward adornment, such as braided hair and the wearing of gold jewelry and fine clothes. Instead, it should be that of your inner self, the unfading beauty of a gentle and quiet spirit, which is of great worth in God's sight.

FOCUS VERSE

Galatians 5:16

Live by the Spirit and you will not gratify the desires of the sinful nature.